David Crockett's Hard-Luck Fate
and Most Fatal Miscalculation of
Joining the Texas Army
That Ordained His Death
at the Alamo

Copyright © 2024 Phillip Thomas Tucker

All rights reserved, including the right to reproduce this book, or portions thereof in any form. No part of this text may be reproduced, transmitted, downloaded, decompiled, reverse engineered, or stored, in any form or introduced into any information storage and retrieval system, in any form or by any means, whether electronic or mechanical without the express written permission of the author.

The views expressed in this work are solely those of the author and do not necessarily reflect the views of the publisher, and the publisher hereby disclaims any responsibility for them.

Cover image:
The Alamo
by TylerEdlinArt, 2009

ISBN: 9798884644137

Also by this author

Nat Turner's Holy War To Destroy Slavery
America's Female Buffalo Soldier: Cathy Williams
Miller Cornfield at Antietam
Pickett's Charge
Death at the Little Bighorn
Barksdale's Charge
Storming Little Round Top
Exodus From The Alamo
Emily D. West and the "Yellow Rose of Texas" Myth
The South's Finest
George Washington's Surprise Attack
How The Irish Won The American Revolution
Why Custer Was Never Warned
The Alamo's Forgotten Defenders
Ranger Raid
Kings Mountain
History of the Irish Brigade
Custer at Gettysburg
The Alamo's Forgotten Defenders
Miller Cornfield at Antietam
America's Hill of Destiny
The Irish in the American Revolution
Irish Confederates
God Help The Irish!
Burnside's Bridge
The Final Fury
Westerners In Gray
Alexander Hamilton's Revolution
The Confederacy's Fighting Chaplain
Cubans In The Confederacy
Forgotten Stonewall of the West
From Auction Block To Glory
The Important Role of the Irish in the American Revolution
The 1862 Plot to Kidnap Jefferson Davis.
Anne Bonny: The Infamous Female Pirate
America's Forgotten First War for Slavery and Genesis of The Alamo
For Honor, Country, and God: Los Niños Héroes
Targeting Abraham: The Forgotten 1865 Plot To Assassinate Lincoln
A New Look at the Buffalo Soldier Experience in Wartime Vol I: Corporal David
Fagen's Metamorphosis and Odyssey
Nanny's War to Destroy Slavery
The Irish at Gettysburg
Blacks in Gray Uniforms
Glory At Fort Wagner: The 54th Massachusetts Vols I, II, and III
Martyred Lieutenant Sanité Bélair
Gran Toya: Founding Mother of Haiti
Claudette Colvin: Forgotten Mother of the Civil Rights Movement
Mulan and the Modern Controversy
Custer's Forgotten Black Soulmate
The Secret Sexual Sins of the Founding Fathers and America: Volumes I and II

Lakshmi Bai
The Trung Sisters
Solitude of Guadeloupe
Daughters of Liberty
Saving Washington's Army
Alexander Hamilton and the Battle of Yorktown
Biden's Folly and America's Turning Point Moment
Biden's Rapid Fall From Grace
Major Robert Rogers and The Racial Dimensions of His Famous 1759 St. Francis Raid
Major Robert Rogers' Tragic Demise
David Fagen: "That Black Devil" of the Philippine-American War
Mary Edmonia Lewis
The Remarkable Story of Little Sister Lozen
Feminism's and Abolitionism's First Tragic Victim: Olympe de Gouges
Josephine Baker: The Forgotten St. Louis Years That Profoundly Shaped Her
Brothers in Liberty
Charlotte L. Forten's Broken Heart
Russian Invasion of Ukraine Leads the World Closer to Nuclear War
Who Killed Custer?
Ida B. Wells
The Wrath of Britain's Celtic Queen Boudica and her Rebellion Against Rome
"Our Marian" Anderson
The Stono Rebellion 1739
Captain Alexander Hamilton's Forgotten Contributions to Decisive Victory at Trenton,
Anne Bonny's Adventures in Jamaica's Waters During Her Last Cruise, Autumn 1720
Anne Bonny Outsmarts the British Legal System in the Courtroom
Anne Bonny's Greatest Exploit
Prince Estabrook
Rommel's Wasted Opportunity to Thwart the D-Day Invasion
Cathy Williams Rises Like a Phoenix from Slavery
The Heroic Revolt of the Trung Sisters
Hitler Orders the Death of Field Marshal Rommel
Anne Bonny's Special Place in History and the Meaning of Courage
Hitler's Ignored Orders That Thwarted His Plan to Stop D-Day Invasion
The Greatest Ambush in History
Demise of the Florida Dream
The Forgotten Black Confederate Fighting Men at the Battle of Painesville, Virginia,
Sophie Scholl: Beheaded by Hitler
Cathy Williams' Struggle Against Racism as America's Female Buffalo Soldier
Black Star-Spangled Hero of Fort McHenry Private William Williams
A Slave Army to Save America in the American Revolution 1779
Napoleon's Descent into the Abyss and Greatest Folly
Bloody October Dawn: Genocide at the Supernova Festival on October 7, 2023
Hitler's Fatal Ignoring of Guderian's Warnings Not to Invade the Soviet Union
Napoleon's Descent into the Abyss and Greatest Folly
The Roman Empire's Internal Collapse
"I Love You to Gaza and Back": The Incredible Story of Israeli Hostage Mia Leimberg
Forgotten Rape of Columbia, South Carolina
The Bloody Hand of Soleimani

David Crockett's Hard-Luck Fate

and Most Fatal Miscalculation of Joining the Texas Army That Ordained His Death at the Alamo

Phillip Thomas Tucker, Ph.D.

Phillip Thomas Tucker, Ph.D. has won recognition as the "Stephen King of History"

Contents

Introduction   1

Chapter I: Plan "To Explore the Texes well before I return" to Tennessee, Autumn of 1835   7

Chapter II: "Land of Milk and Honey," Texas   43

Chapter III: Doomed at the Alamo   55

Epilogue   69

Bibliography   71

About the Author   73

Introduction

Why another book about David Crockett at this late date in the twenty-first century? Crockett has been the central figure of any and every book and Hollywood movie about the Alamo decade after decade. He became not only a Texas revolutionary but also a national martyr and hero, after he was killed at the Alamo by soldiers of the Republic of Mexico on the early morning darkness of March 6, 1836.

First and foremost, instead of the usual glorification of Crockett as the "King of the Wild Frontier," former Tennessee Congressman, a common soldier of the Creek War of 1813-1814, and the Texas Revolution of 1836, this book will present a more realistic, honest, and even contrarian look at Crockett by penetrating through the dense layers of myths and legends about the popular Tennessean that seemed to have no end to present a more honest and realistic look at him.

In consequence and for the most part, the thesis of this current book might well be described as the hard luck story about Crockett's life, which was the antithesis of the standard and traditional glorious portrayal of his life, because what has been presented in this work has been basically the fundamental truths, including dark ones, about the difficult and hardscrabble life of a poor man from the beginning to the end. It is somewhat of a classic paradox that Crockett's life has been catapulted into a celebrated and glorious chapter of American history in the twentieth century more than a century after he was killed at the Alamo largely for political reasons.

And, of course, the most famous example of Crockett's hard luck and difficult life can best be seen in the final chapter of his life, the Texas Revolutionary period of 1835-1836. The call of large quantities of free land in Texas beckoned him and friends from their Weakley County homes in northwest Tennessee in the autumn of 1835 to embark upon the pursuit of the American Dream, which was then located in Texas. Dictated by his hard-luck and ill-fate, this final odyssey of Crockett's life led to his entry into the Texas Army and a people's revolution in which he met his doom at the Alamo on the early morning of March 6, 1836, just when he believed that he had finally turned a major corner in his life for the better.

After Crockett and a small party of friends explored the unspoiled countryside of east Texas which was the reason they had departed Tennessee and he then joined the Texas Army on February 8, 1836 and less than a month before the Alamo fell, famous Tennessee frontiersmen seemed destined to finally claim his large number of Texas acres on August 8, when his six month term of service expired. Indeed, just when the fighting of the Texas Revolution seemed over when the last Mexican soldier had been forced out of Texas in December 1835 and the war seemingly had been won by early 1836, it seemed as if Crockett would see no fighting, when he and his "Tennessee Volunteers" were stationed with the small Anglo-Celtic garrison at San Antonio de Bexar, located on the Central Plains of Texas and near the old Spanish mission called the Alamo.

However, everything suddenly changed and dramatically so when President Lopez de Santa Anna led a large Mexican Army north and caught the Anglo-Celtic garrison by surprise. They hurriedly evacuated San Antonio de Bexar and fled into the safety of the ill-prepared Alamo in a narrow escape. Indeed, they were lucky to have escaped with their lives. However, the Alamo was nothing more than a death-trap for the tiny garrison of less than 200 men, including of course Crockett. At this time, Crockett found himself at exactly the wrong place at the wrong time, after the Alamo was quickly surrounded by the large Mexican Army under Santa Anna, whose mostly of Aztec heritage and mixed-race soldiers wore Napoleonic uniforms of old: a situation that was true to the past course of Crockett's difficult and tough course of the Tennessean's hard-luck life. Clearly, Crockett's luck remained extremely bad in Texas and destiny stayed a dark one for him until his dying day on the early bloody morning of March 6, when Santa Anna unleashed his surprise attack that caught the garrison completely by surprise in the darkness.

Clearly, in the end, an unkind fate continued to dominate Crockett's hardscrabble life and it was one that he could never escape no matter how hard he tried. Like the rest of the Alamo defenders before the arrival of daylight, he was killed in the stealthy early morning Mexican attack when the garrison fell to the last man, because of Santa Anna's no quarter policy. However, to this day, no one knows of the exact manner of Crockett's death because no one among the Anglo-Celtic garrison survived the slaughter, because Santa Anna's war was one of no mercy. For decades afterward, wild stories circulated that Crockett had escaped the massacre and that he was still alive, including allegedly laboring year after year as a slave in a Mexican silver mine.

But, of course, these were just idle rumors without any foundation whatsoever, because the romantic legend of Crockett never died as it was too large to fade away and die. But, of course, Crockett died on the bloody morning of March 6 and his remains and bones were cremated outside of the Alamo's walls in one of the three funeral pyres upon the Alamo dead had been placed by the victors. Then, his resilient legend was resurrected and continued to live on when it brought to life by the Disney Corporation and Hollywood for the "Baby Boom" generation of the 1950s during the Cold War, when America needed to celebrate its heroes, which led to a recreation of Crockett into a great national idol and hero more than a century after his death. Of course, no one would have been more surprised by this development than Crockett.

But, in the end and in truth, there was little that was glamorous or romantic about Crockett's life and especially his death far from home and family since he was the victim of a massacre. Clearly, this was a tragic and sad fate of an American icon and hero who was killed in a foreign land, owned by the Republic of Mexico, far from home and one not of his birth and hardly even of his understanding, while serving as a rebel—Santa Anna called them land pirates—in the uprising against the Republic of Mexico. As an Indian fighter and lowly common soldier under General Andy Jackson during the Creek War without high rank and then a Tennessee Congressman in Washington, D.C., Crockett had been one of the most talked about and popular men of his generation across the United States, when he committed the folly of deciding to enter the Texas Army mainly because the lust for large amount of land were irresistible to a poor man. Tragically, from the beginning, a harsh fate and destiny had ordained that Crockett departed his northwest Tennessee homeland, which he would never see again, in the fall of 1835 to journey southwest far from family to die in a strange land to which he was a perfect stranger to meet his Maker at the Alamo in a sad and tragic irony.

Besides the factor of hard luck life of a poor man in a difficult life from beginning to end, Crockett had been forced all of his life to stay on the move in search of the elusive American Dream just like his hardscrabble ancestors going back generations: the very reason why he ended up at the Alamo in far-away Texas at the ripe age of forty-nine in the hope of starting over again to build a new life for himself and his family in Texas for brighter days in the future. However, in the end, Crockett was trapped at the Alamo with the small garrison of Anglo-Celts because he had too often tempted fate in the past, while also losing his risky Texas gamble to gain personal and political renewal (he had lost his seat in Congress in August 1835) and prosperity, especially in the form of land, in a new land far from Tennessee. Unfortunate, and like for other doomed men at the Alamo, it was not to be for Crockett, who lost his life in making his risky last gamble of his hard luck life. He never returned to see his friends, wife and family, and far-away home ever again in far-away Tennessee, because of his relentless search of the American Dream that always seemed to be always out-of-reach and lay over the next distant horizon.

In this current book, I will not cover the Battle of the Alamo in any great detail, because I already achieved that objective in my groundbreaking 2010 book *Exodus from the Alamo, the Anatomy of the Last Stand Myth*, which presented a great many new insights and views about one of the most famous battles in the annals of American history. Again, this current book is not focused on the familiar and well-known story of the Alamo that has been so often retold for generations. In fact, this current book, published in 2024, is quite contrarian compared to any look at David Crockett, who has continued to be celebrated and glorified by modern historians to this day.

Phillip Thomas Tucker, Ph.D.
Central Florida
January 16, 2023

Chapter I

Plan "To Explore the Texes well before I return" to Tennessee, Autumn of 1835

The hasty, last-minute decision at Nacogdoches, located in east Texas and generally considered the oldest town in Texas, to join the Texas Revolutionary Army on January 14, 1836 sealed the fate of David Crockett. He would never again see his home and family. This was Crockett's first experience in the extremely dangerous business of engaging in revolution on the soil of another country and a foreign power, the Republic of Mexico. Crockett eventually realized that he had made a grave mistake, but only when it was far too late.

When Crockett and a few friends and a nephew departed the worn lands of northwest Tennessee in Weakley County, which had a northern border with Kentucky, around the beginning of November 1835, he had no intention of joining a people's revolution far from his northwestern Tennessee home, which was contrary to the romantic myth. This former Tennessee Congressman of French Huguenot and Irish descent was going to Texas in search of rich and fertile land to settle his family and his friends. As he had written just before he departed for the distant land of Texas far to the southwest about his main objective of riding all the way to Texas: "to explore the Texes well before I return" to the arms of his loving family, which included his second wife Elizabeth Patton-Crockett, in northwest Tennessee, where the land was drained by the North, Middle, and South Forks of the Obion River to eventually enter the Mississippi River to the west. The unusual name of Obion was a corruption of the name of an early Scotch-Irish trapper and fur trader named O'Brien or O'Bion. For Crockett and his friends, the trip to Texas was little more than a hunting expedition and they set out with the intention of exploring Texas for future settlement and nothing more.

    Although he might not have been aware for the full extent of the danger on January 14, 1836 when he took the Texas oath primarily because the last armed Mexican soldados, or soldiers, already had been forced out of Texas in December 1835 and it then seemed as if the brief war of 1835 between the Anglo-Texas settlers and the soldiers of the Republic of Mexico was over, Crockett's abrupt decision to join a common people's revolutionary army in the nineteenth century was a risky gamble. The Texas Revolutionary Army was a motley collection of volunteers with little military experience. Most of all, Crocket was determined to obtain a good many prime Texas acres for his six-month period of service in the Volunteer Auxiliary Corps of the Texas Army. Without a moment's hesitation, he was risking his life for the golden opportunity to gain those large number of Texas acres by fighting Mexicans and, of course, he might well get killed in the process. Of course, this was certainly not in Crockett's game plan, which would thwart his lofty ambitions to resettle his family and friends on thousands of prime acres in Texas, when they were depending on him back home. Instead and most of all, he was hoping to survive his term of military service and revive his political fortunes—which would be very easy to accomplish in this new land since everyone from the United States and transplanted United States citizens in Texas knew his name—by becoming a delegate to the upcoming constitution at Washington-on-the-Brazos, Texas, which served as the rustic capital of the Stephen Fuller Austin Colony of Anglo-Celts. However, once on Texas soil, Crockett soon discovered that he was ineligible to become a delegate since he had just reached Texas and was not yet a permanent settler. Therefore, to aspire higher in life and out of default, Crockett would have to serve out his six-months terms of service in the Texas Army to acquire his nice bounty of thousands of Texas acres. As fate would have it and with his political ambitions now thwarted in both the United States in losing his Congressional seat 1835 and the new revolutionary government of Texas in 1836 in relatively short order to his dismay and frustration, the newly-enlisted Crockett shortly learned after all that he would have to risk his life when facing a mighty army from Mexico, while hoping to survive the war to collect his thousands of Texas acres for the settlement of his family and friends.

Perhaps no one said it better about the high risks of joining a people's revolution than sage Benjamin Franklin, who not long after the signing of the Declaration of

Independence in Philadelphia, Pennsylvania, had emphasized a truism when reminding his fellow delegates of the great risks in waging war against the British Empire, which was the most powerful on earth: "We must all hang together, most assuredly, or, we shall all hung separately." Clearly, Frankin, who was one of America's leading founding fathers, fully understood the high risks of the colonists, who were amateurs at war, engaging in revolution against a powerful nation that was the mother country of England. Ironically, David Crockett, who had been born in a remote place called Limestone on the Nolichucky River in east Tennessee, on August 17, 1786 and whose father had served in the American Revolution, did not learn about this fundamental reality until it was far too late.

Indeed, in rebelling against King George III and a mighty empire beginning in April 1775, these true rustics and amateurs in rebellion, including the founding fathers, were now inexperienced revolutionaries—like the Texas colonists--risking their lives in having decided to take on mighty England, because they believed in the Dream of America and its future greatness could be obtained by reaching out and grabbing it, if the American revolutionaries could only break the shackles of the mother country. Clearly, this was a great gamble and the risk of becoming a revolutionary against a powerful mother country, but the founding fathers and colonial Americans prevailed against the odds in the end, winning independence in 1783. Across the Atlantic, generations of

Irish and Scotsmen, like fiery revolutionary leader William Wallace, had failed to prevail in their own nationalistic struggles in their Celtic homelands against the considerable might of England over the centuries. In fact, Ireland became England's first colony in the 1600s and the Irish people suffered severely as the conquered ones of their own homeland and who had been thoroughly subjugated by the British and would remain so for centuries.

The astounding closeness that America came to nearly losing the American Revolution was truly astounding and little realized or fully understood by Americans today. It was indeed a very close call for the upstart republic of outgunned and outclassed revolutionaries. In fact, the novice Americans, who had to create a government, army, and navy from scratch, would have certainly lost their struggle for liberty against the odds had not the mighty French Army and Navy of the Gallic nation—the historic archenemy of England for centuries—come to the rescue in timely fashion. Everything changed for America when France signed the French Alliance with the revolutionaries in 1778. Thankfully, the French joined with the Americans in an all-important alliance (that had its ups and down partly because France had been America's enemy during the French and Indian War and because the English colonies had been long dragged into the international conflicts of Europe for generations before the American Revolution) against England, which eventually resulted in the remarkable Allied victory by forcing the surrender of British-Hessian-Loyalist army of Lord Charles Cornwallis at Yorktown, Virginia, in October 1781, and then the peace settlement of 1783, the Treaty of Paris.

In early October 1835 and as mentioned, yet another people's revolution of amateurs broke out among the feisty Anglo-Celtic settlers in the northeastern province owned by the Republic of Mexico, which had won its independence from Spain in 1821. Ironically, both American and Mexico were revolutionary republics and neighbors, who had defeated their European masters. And now the "Texican" colonists were attempting to create their own people's republic just like their revolutionary forefathers, including Crockett's own father who fought with distinction at the Battle of Kings Mountain, South Carolina, on October 7, 1780, which changed the course of the American Revolution during some of the darkest days of the struggle for independence. Like his son, the father was also a poor frontiersman and hardscrabble farmer of the lower-class or lower middle-class at best.

Like Spain before it, Mexico had committed the same folly that was foolishly allowing large numbers of Anglo-Celts from the United States to settle in Texas in the hope that they could develop and turn it into a land of promise instead of an unproductive, underdeveloped one. Mexico had miscalculated badly and was destined to pay a high price for its miscalculation that was absolute folly. Incredibly, Mexican political leadership believed that these free-thinking Protestant settlers would willingly convert to Catholicism and then become good and peaceful citizens of the Republic of Mexico, once they had been allowed to settle in Texas with the granting of bountiful acreage to them. Of course, the vast majority of Protestants and Anglo-Celts who settled in Texas had no desire to forsake their religion or live under an authoritarian and dictatorial government, which was the antithesis of the kind of free and independent life that they had left behind in the United States.

At first to government leaders of Spain and then Mexico, it was hoped that the Anglo-Celtic settlers would turn their backs on their revered political, social, religious, and cultural antecedents—an impossibility of course and including their introduction of slavery into Texas (Mexico had freed its slaves in 1829) which was badly needed to develop this raw, fertile region—and tame the wild lands of Texas to make this northeastern province of Mexico with endless potential prosperous a lucrative asset to the Latino republic. Of course as could be expected, this overly optimistic and impractical strategy of Mexico backfired for a host of reasons, but primarily because the Anglo-Celts, including immigrants from Ireland, were determined to live in the manner of a liberal republic like in the United States instead of cowering under the arbitrary and heavy-handed dictates of a centralized authoritarian regime ruled by the entrenched elites of Mexico City. The settlers also cherished the right of revolution to redress a government's wrongs since they believed that it was a people's right to do so, just like their revolutionary forefathers which was a revered heritage from both sides of the Atlantic.

Like in the case of the American Revolution, for the relatively few settlers to embark upon the task of waging revolution against an established foreign power from scratch was a great risk, because Mexican was far more powerful and populous than the small Stephen Fuller Austin Colony of Texas. In consequence after the first fight erupted between the colonists and Mexican military at the tiny community of Gonzales, Texas, which was known as the "Lexington of Texas," on October 2, 1835, the nascent Texas Revolution had desperately needed to quickly recruit a people's army to hurl Mexican troops from Texas. Almost immediately, therefore, the word spread across the United States that Texas needed volunteers, who would be rewarded with large numbers of Texas acres—actually the acreage of the Republic of Mexico that was only the rebel's own if the Anglo-Celts won the revolution. However, in isolated and remote northwest Tennessee, Crockett had not heard about the outbreak of the Texas Revolution, when he and his friends and nephew departed for Texas in early November 1835. As noted, he had no desire to go to war with anyone, especially the Republic of Mexico. At this time in his life at age forty-nine, Crockett was now far more of a popular politician than a fighter and he had already seen enough warfare for one lifetime during the Creek War of 1813-1814.

At this time, Crockett was a man who could not have been more disillusioned with life in the United States, especially in the political realm that had turned to reject him. He had just lost his Tennessee seat in the United States

Congress, in August 1835 having been voted out of Congress by his frontier constituents of the Obion River country in northwest Tennessee. He had lost out to a wealthier and better educated political opponent gifted with a smoother tongue and supported by the powerful political machine of the ever-popular President Andrew Jackson, who was America's great hero of the War of 1812. Crockett was disgusted with politics and even more disgusted with Jackson's authoritarian ways (he was considered a dictator by his political opposition) that had caused the native South Carolinian to be looked at as a non-republican. Crockett had famously already told his constituents of his district in northwest Tennessee of the fateful decision that would take him to his grave: "I told the people of my district that I would serve them as faithfully as I had done; but if not [and if voted out of office then] you may all go to hell, and I will go to Texas."

However, these well-known words of the celebrated frontiersman from Tennessee were said in the days before the outbreak of the Texas Revolution at Gonzales, when the defiant colonists raised the revolutionary banner "Come and Take It," which symbolized their refusal to relinquish a small cannon back to Mexican authorities and a small detachment of Mexican cavalrymen that had demanded its return under threat of military action. The first clash of the Texas Revolution occurred on October 2, 1835, when Mexican cavalrymen predictably attempted to take the gun by force, which then ignited the spark of a fiery people's revolution. It was the folly of an inexperienced and overconfident revolutionary leadership, which was divided in its strategic thinking and divergent ambitions in a chaotic situation, that set the stage for the taking of Crockett's life in the end.

As mentioned, Crockett and his friends did not ride hundreds of miles all the way from northwest Tennessee and through mostly Arkansas to just lose their lives in fighting in the Texas Revolution. In Crockett's words about his main objective, and as mentioned, just before his departure from home that fully revealed the truth of what drove him to Texas and it was certainly not the Texas Revolution: "to explore Texes well before I return" home to Weakley County, Tennessee. This was contrary to the popular romantic myth, which was first perpetuated by Hollywood, especially Disney Productions because of its excessive and over the top portrayal and glorification of Crockett, who was transformed into a national icon and idol during the Cold War period of the 1950s. This fanciful modern mythmaking fueled by Hollywood and especially by the 1955 release of Disney's *Davy Crockett, King of the Wild Frontier* was in perfectly keeping with the day's Cold War patriotism when America needed heroes to be revered and celebrated, including by the youngsters of the "Baby Boom," whose fathers had fought in and played their part in winning the Second World War. As noted, the opportunity to visit Texas became a reality for Crockett in August 1835, when he lost his Congressional seat in Washington, D.C., and now, "I will go to Texas."

Excessively embellished by Alamo films, especially John Wayne's Hollywood excessively fanciful production of *The Alamo* of 1960, the myth was created by Hollywood and Disney that Crockett's sole purpose of journeying to Texas was to fight for the new Texas republic, against the despotism of Mexico, and for the freedom the Anglo-Celts in Texas, which was simply not the case. Even more, this standard romanticized and glorified portrayal of Crockett has completely overlooked the rather disturbing fact that Crockett would in fact be fighting for a robust slave society and republic, whose economy resulted solidly on the institution of slavery just like in the Deep South to the east.

This traditional simplistic scenario of Hollywood having Crockett solely battling for freedom in the name of American patriotism has certainly made for a nice story and a rousing patriotic tale in past decades, but it was simply untrue and nothing more than fantasy. It was true that the Texas settlers in revolution were mostly poor frontier people, mostly from the South, like Crockett, including many of his fellow Tennesseans, but going to war against Mexico was never a reason for Crockett's long journey southwest all the way to east Texas, which was merely a social and economic extension of the slave-owning South. Again, this alleged primary motivation of Crockett's excessive patriotism and love for republicanism to explain his going to Texas was nothing more than a romantic fable and myth created by Hollywood scriptwriters, which amazingly has endured to this day.

In truth and as noted, what Crockett was looking for by going to Texas was nothing more than a search for good hunting grounds and new fertile lands for the future settlement of his family and neighbors. He certainly did not ride so far southwest to risk and perhaps lose his life in a shooting war that was the Texas Revolution against a powerful nation. At this time, the American Dream equated to acquiring large amounts of land in Texas in the tradition of a wealthy elites having acquired extensive Southern plantations, which was something that no Crockett had previously secured generation after generation. And Crockett and his people were true blue Southerners of the Upper South located in the lands just east of the Mississippi River. And the only way that a poor American in 1835 could secure large amounts of land was to obtain it in Texas and especially by enlisting in Texas military service, after the Texas Revolution erupted in early October 1835.

Despite having served as a Tennessee Congressman in Washington, D.C., who had partly campaigned on his Creek War record of 1813-1814, until voted out of office in August 1835 and had acquired national fame across America from his political campaigns when he had been the consummate showman with his own unique set of humor-laced theatrics and outrageous tall tales, Crockett was still a poor man in 1835 because he, like his ancestors, had never acquired large numbers of acres. He had plenty of ups and downs in life, including losing bids for the House of Representatives in 1825 and 1831, but he won in 1827, 1829, and 1833 to represent Tennessee. But as noted,

Crockett finally lost his final bid for a Congressional seat in the summer of 1835, which set the stage for him and his friends to ride southwest to Texas to search for a new beginning and a better life, which set the stage for his death at the Alamo in early March 1836. And through it all and over the decades, he was never able to make it big and this ill-fate continued to the very end, dying at the Alamo as a poor man without ever owning the large number of Texas acres that he coveted and had risked his life to obtain for himself and his family.

Before the Texas Revolution

In consequence, by the fall of 1835, Crockett was still exactly the same that he had been before he had embarked upon a political career as a Tennessee Congressman: a poor frontiersman who was engaged in non-ceasing search of a better life and brighter future, which was basically the American Dream. Ironically, Crockett had not even significantly benefitted from one of the largest land grabs in American history as the result of a conflict in which he had fought and risked his life many times, the Creek War of 1813-1814. The great dream of the wealthy Southern planter class, which had long lusted for the rich lands (today's Alabama, Georgia, and Mississippi) to be stripped away the Creek people, finally became reality when the militant Redsticks of the Creek Nation lost their war for independence. Indeed, from the beginning for whites of all classes, the Creek War was all about stealing the rich lands of the Creeks under the guise of Manifest Destiny. Since Crockett had not benefitted from his war service by not acquiring a large amount of Creek lands taken by the United States after the defeat of the Creeks, the only other option for him was to acquire the American Dream was to go to Texas.

For years, the large slave-owners and wealthy plantation owners across the South had long desired war with the Creeks, or the Muskogee people, to secure their native homeland that covered most of the Southeast, wishing for the golden opportunity to start a war that would push the Creeks off their ancestral lands. As a true Tennessean of the Volunteer State, Crockett grabbed his flintlock musket after receiving the shocking news of the "massacre" by around 700 Creek Redsticks and black warriors, who had been former slaves, of whites and "half-breeds" at a small fort in the Mobile country not far north of the Gulf of Mexico. The news of the Fort Mims massacre shocked the settlers of the Southeast and Upper South to fuel the desire for revenge. In Crockett's words: "The truth is, my dander was up and nothing but war could bring it right again." Crockett's vindictive words were representative of the volunteers who flocked to the ranks of the Tennessee militia. But as in most wars, the Creek War was a rich man's war, but a poor man's fight. Crockett was one of those poor men from the South with a lowly rank unlike the wealthy, aristocratic elites, including slaveowners of the wealthy planter class, who served as officers of the Tennessee militia.

The Redsticks under Red Eagle, the fieriest and most militant of the Creek war chiefs, had been emboldened by the spirit of nationalism and having been told by the Creek shamans that they were immune to the white man's bullets, had struck Fort Mims with a vengeance. Around 250 whites and "half-breeds" were attacked by Red Eagle at Fort Mims on Lake Tensaw in the then Mississippi Territory. The so-called fort that housed fearful local settlers was located around forty miles northeast of the Gulf of Mexico port of Mobile. For Mims was attacked on August 30, 1813 by Red Stick Creeks and the Southeast would never been the same. Red Eagle's warriors had adhered to the words of their pro-war prophets who promised victory in a great spiritual uprising and sacred revolt against the white interlopers. The Redsticks were the war faction of the Creek nation that was badly divided between peace and war in a true civil war. Fueled by their religions and shamans, the Creeks waged an unconditional holy war and a religious revolution, since they were fighting against the escalation of a steady white encroachment, American colonialism, and the march of Manifest Destiny deeper into the Southeast, while attempting to preserve their way of life and sacred traditions of their cherished ancestors.

In addition, the Creeks had plenty of old scores to settle with the whites. White encroachment had already resulted in the Creeks having lost millions of precious acres of some of their best hunting grounds that had been lost forever, when they struck back in anger beginning at Fort Mims. Most of all, the Creeks wanted to restore their former traditional way-of-life and regain their former lands that were being continuously lost under the constant pressure of the white avalanche of settlers. And now the slaughter at Fort Mims had now given the white planter class and the wealthy slave-owning elites the long-awaited excuse to send a volunteer army into the heart of Creek country and acquire Creek lands by force for the creation of an empire for slavery on the rich lands taken from the Creeks.

And this war was more complex than most Indian wars because this conflict was also about slavery to a surprising degree, which has been generally forgotten. For generations, escaped slaves had fled south and joined with the Creeks to fight for their freedom, while wealthy Americans not only wanted to expand an empire for slavery to increase their riches, but also to regain their escaped slaves and eliminate the threat of escaping slaves and those rising up in revolt. The *South Carolina Gazette* of Charles Town (today's Charleston) reported that as early as between the period of 1732 and 1752 (owners offered nice financial rewards for escaped slaves) some "679 Negro slaves" had fled to the lands of the Muskogees or Creeks. In an indirect sense and way, Crockett and his Creek War comrades partly fought for a new land of slavery, the enslavement of escaped slaves, and the establishment of future cotton plantations, which they could never own for themselves because they were poor men, in today's Georgia, Mississippi, and Alabama.

This was prime cotton country, which was later known as the fertile Black Belt because of the richness of the soil.

So, the Creek War was also very much about the issue of slavery: 1) keeping the "peculiar" institution safe and secure from the slashing Creek attacks into the farmlands and plantations of the settlers who had already taken former Native American hunting grounds, and, 2) stopping an exodus of slaves, including those freed in Creek raids, to the Creeks, who saw them as kindred spirits and fellow fighting against the menace of white encroachment on Indian lands, because the former slaves formed a diehard core of resistance against the Americans because they feared enslavement.

And whites of all classes also partly fought for the capture and return to slavery of the hundreds of slaves who had escaped to the Creek for decades. The blacks living with the Creeks as free people were seen by whites as a constant threat, especially by the planter class, that needed to be eliminated. In wartime, the blacks served as the faithful allies of the Creeks and later the Seminoles in Florida. They became known as some of the most fierce and best fighting men of the Creek War and later the series of Seminole War, including the first battle that erupted in December 1835, when Major Francis L. Dade and more than one hundred of his United States regulars were massacred partly by former slaves. Of course, these ex-slaves possessed an urgent need to play an extremely active part in stopping white expansion into Creek lands, which were also their homeland where they enjoyed sweet freedom. If these former slaves were recaptured by the whites, then a lifetime of slavery awaited them. Even more, whites worried that the combined black warriors and Redstick Creeks would wage an aggressive and effective war against white plantations across the South in a war against slavery that would hurl back white settlement in the Southeast.

But yet a pressing international factor came into play that also was a key equation in the Creek War. The Creeks had long secured black powder and weapons from the Spanish governor in Pensacola, Florida. Pensacola was a vital strategic port located on the northern side of the Gulf of Mexico and the largest Spanish port in the Gulf of Mexico. Here, at the picturesque port with a beautiful, wide natural harbor that led to the Gulf of Mexico, the Spanish governor ruled the vast territory of Spanish Florida, that was little more than a sprawling wilderness. The Spanish were chief suppliers, including also weapons and munitions gained from British trading firms, for war supplies that enabled the Creeks to raid white settlements and wage war. Long angering the settlers in the Southeast, this situation was especially the case during the War of 1812 and in the Creek War from 1812-1813. This key factor provided another reason why war needed to be waged against these two foreign threats dominating the Gulf of Mexico region, because the British and Spanish were allies during the War of 1812, which posed a great threat to America, especially for the settlers living on the isolated Georgia, Alabama, Mississippi, and Florida frontiers.

Still another factor played a role in the rising up of the ultra-nationalist Creeks, or the Red Sticks. This was the rise of not only nationalism but also war fever fueled by the concept of a Pan-Native Americanism that had been spread by Tecumseh, who had close contracts with high-ranking British officers in Detroit on Lake Michigan in today's Michigan. A revered Shawnee chief born in the Ohio country and whose father, like other relatives, had been killed in battle against the Americans in 1774, Tecumseh was an ultra-nationalist war chief who attempted to unite all of the tribes, including the Creeks who he had visited to win their support, in an organized resistance effort to stop the omnipresent white expansion. He was a true nationalist and the most influential and powerful advocate of pan-Indian resistance to unite all Native American people against the whites in a holy war that would be raised across the North American continent. Tecumseh's fiery nationalist message reached a ready audience, especially among the Redstick Creeks. In Tecumseh's words spoken to unite all Indian peoples together as one against the interloping, land-hungry Americans, whose lust for Indian lands was limitless: "Let the white race perish; The seize your land; They corrupt your women, they trample on the ashes of your dead! Back whence they came, upon a trail of blood, they must be driven."

Tecumseh's great dream of Pan-Native Americanism died when he was killed by American soldiers at the Battle of the Thames in Canada on October 5, 1813. In the midst of the War of 1812, Americans had amply justification to be worried for national security reasons because of Tecumseh's efforts and the interference of the British and

Spanish to push the Creeks to war with the Americans, which placed the entire Southern frontier in jeopardy. The Creeks had only planned to rise up en masse if Tecumseh won victory in the North, but the warlike Redstick faction could no longer wait for Tecumseh, while white encroachment continued to increase and more white injustices were committed against them in their own invaded homeland, while more prime hunting grounds were lost with each passing day. Hence, Red Eagle's attack on Fort Mims was so devastating because he was fueled by Tecumseh's great dream and had caught the garrison by surprise.

In his eagerness to answer his country's call, Crockett was one of the first to volunteer for militia service in the Creek War. Crockett's joining up with enthusiasm was part of a flood for volunteers who filled the ranks of the Tennessee militia. With the news of the Fort Mims "massacre" that guaranteed the entry of the United States military into the bitter Creek civil war, the governors of Tennessee, Georgia and the Mississippi Territory called out the militia. Now up in arms, the South was outraged and motivated by the war cry of "Remember Fort Mims." At a time when Southern newspapers called for the "extermination" of the Creeks, Andrew Jackson was appointed by Tennessee Governor William Blout, who had been born in North Carolina and served in the North Carolina militia during the American Revolution, to command the Tennessee Volunteers to march south into the depths of Creek country. The irrepressible Jackson, of

Scotch-Irish descent, became the right-hand man of Governor Blout and they were a highly effective leadership team. A veteran of the Revolutionary War during which almost all Native American tribes had sided with the British, Jackson proved to the most remarkable military man in the history of the Southeast, which he won practically on his own with relatively few troops in hard-hitting campaigns that were as remarkable as they were epic.

Knowing that the Creeks were supported by both the British from their warships and Spain, principally from Pensacola, Jackson was ruthless because he realized that the future of the entire Southeast was at stake. In no uncertain terms, he emphasized how "revenge" was now the order of the day, which fueled his fierce determination that the "whole Creek nation shall be covered with blood." In consequence, the one-sided Creek War witnessed one massacre of Creeks after another by the unleashed Americans, because the Creeks were so badly mismatched with only about a third of the warriors possessing firearms. They never had a chance against the well-armed Americans, especially the frontiersmen, under the hard-hitting Jackson. In this most brutal of wars, American victories were nothing more than massacres in what was basically a true racial war. Perhaps Tennessee Governor William Blount said it best regarding the general feelings of whites, both civilians and soldiers at this time, and the typical mentality of the day about the need "to teach those barbarous sons of their woods their inferiority."

Enlisting for six months term of service at Winchester, Franklin County, Tennessee, just north of the Alabama Territory on September 24, 1813, young Tennessee volunteer David Crockett was a true patriot who served in the ranks of Captain Francis Jones's Company of Tennessee Volunteers of Mounted Rifles. He left behind wife Mary Polly Finley, of Scotch-Irish descent who he had married in 1806, and his children at a small farm south of Winchester to go to war against the Creeks. Fearful of losing a husband and main provider, Polly begged her husband not to go and leave the family behind, but Crockett was determined to go in part because of his wandering nature and, most of all, a burning desire to protect white settlers, who were a poor people living on the remote frontier like himself.

In Crockett's own words: "My countrymen had been murdered, and I know that the next thing would be, that the Indians would be scalping the women and children all about there [in Tennessee], if we don't put a stop to it." This was the typical frontier attitude of taking matters into their own hands like seen with the sparkling Patriot victory over the Loyalists at Kings Mountain in October 1780 during the American Revolution, especially when it came to matters of home defense. The frontiersmen were determined to do what had to be done in a matter of fact and commonsense manner that was very much Darwinian in a dangerous frontier environment. Crockett's mounted company, under Captain Jones, became part of the Tennessee command under Virginia-born Colonel John Coffee, who was one of the most capable cavalry commanders in the land and the top lieutenant of General Jackson.

At the time of the slaughter at Fort Mims, Jackson was still recovering from a near fatal pistol wound in the left arm that he had suffered during a wild melee with his political enemies in Nashville's dusty streets on September 4, nearly dying in bed from the serious wound. But in a remarkable development, he somehow mustered the strength and stamina to depart Nashville, which was Tennessee's rough-and-tumble capital, and join Colonel Coffee, who had been awaiting his arrival before pushing forward into Creek country, on October 24, 1813. With the pistol ball still lodged deep in his left arm, Jackson had jumped out of bed hastened south because of recent alarming news from Coffee.

This alarming news had been gained by Crockett and other scouts, who were the best woodsmen of the mounted volunteer company of Captain Jones and who had been earlier dispatched as scouts by Colonel Coffee, that the Red Sticks were pushing north toward southern Tennessee. Colonel Coffee, with Crockett in the mounted ranks, then led General Jackson's advance south into Creek country with the determination to avenge what had happened at Fort Mims. Jackson's having taken the field with an unhealed arm wound became one reason why his men later gave him the on-target name of "Old Hickory," because his toughness that even amazed his hardened frontiersmen and which became legendary in the Creek War.

Crockett was determined to fight and risk his life in the Creek War to protect the settlers of the South, but also, he felt a surprising degree of compassion for the Creek people, because they were losing not only their ancestral lands, but also their way of life in a mismatch on the field of strife. And they were a weaker, underdog people, who possessed less firearms than the Americans and believed that they were immune to white bullets, which, of course, they learned otherwise the hard way. The Creek War was one about not only ethnic cleansing but also about genocide to wipe clean the Creek homeland of its inhabitants that was first required before the establishment of a thriving cotton kingdom.

American victories were basically nothing more than slaughters and massacres to the extent that the killing of a racial war even sickened Crockett, who was a hardened frontiersman, and other militiamen, because of the bloodletting. In the ranks with around 900 comrades who had surrounded the sleeping Creek village before the break of dawn, Crockett participated in Coffee's massacre of the unfortunate inhabitants of the Creek village at Tallushatchee in the Mississippi Territory on November 3, 1813. This was Jackson's first victory of the Creek War, and it was little more than a gory massacre. Crockett later wrote how: "We shot them down like dogs" without mercy at Tallushatchee that had become a great killing field.

When around 50 Creek warriors took refuge in a log house and fought tenaciously from it, Coffee ordered the wooden structure to be fired, ensuring the end of resistance in horrific fashion with the trapped Indians singing their death songs and screaming in pain amid the roaring flames. Later, Crockett and his comrades, who were starving because of logistical breakdowns of Jackson's Army that was not well organized in the frantic rush to invade the Creek homeland, found a potato cellar under the ashes of the house and feasted on the cooked potatoes from "the oil of the [burned alive] Indians . . . had run down on them, and they looked like they had been stewed with fat meat." Crockett's hunger was so great that he never before had more thoroughly enjoyed the taste of roast potatoes in his life.

More than 200 Creeks at Tullushatchee were killed in the gory slaughter, including women and children. But at least around eighty women and children were taken prisoner instead of being killed on the spot, which revealed that Jackson was not entirely ruthless and not a stereotypical advocate of genocide, as has been often claimed today by liberal historians, who had generally looked upon him as a great Indian killer driven by blood lust: a popular myth that has become popular in recent decades. By far, this was truer regarding Native American warriors rather than women and children, who bore the brunt of Jackson's wrath. He even saved a Creek child whose parents had been killed at Tullushatchee. As a man who had been orphaned in the American Revolution, Jackson identified with the infant and adopted him as a son for him and wife Rachel. Lyncoya was raised with loving care at Jackson's Hermitage located just outside Nashville.

Clearly, Jackson was a complex man, who saw himself as doing what was necessary to save American settlers and the Southeast, which posed a serious omnipresent threat because of the British and Spanish presence along the Gulf of Mexico in wartime.

A few days after the Tullushatchee massacre, General Jackson learned that many of the friendly Creeks of this bitter civil war were being besieged by Redsticks at Talladega. He immediately dispatched Colonel Coffee and his mounted volunteers, including Crockett, to the rescue on the double. The Redsticks were surrounded by Coffee and around 300 Redsticks were killed during the fighting on November 9 in relieving the siege at the small loss of only around fifteen men. After this one-sided victory and because of logistical reasons and the need for Coffee's command to refit and recuperate from rough campaigning deep in the wilderness of the Creek country, Jackson ordered Coffee and his men to return to Nashville. This first phase of Crockett's campaigning during the War of 1812 was over. In a happy reunion, Crockett returned to wife Polly's and his family's arms after having been discharged on Christmas Eve 1813.

But the war called "America's Second War of Independence," the War of 1812, was far from over. Determined to reap his revenge after surrounding the major Redstick village of Tohopeka, General Jackson then decisively defeated the Redstick Creeks at the Battle of Horseshoe Bend on the chocolate-colored Tallapoosa River on March 27, 1814. The defiant warriors defended the narrow neck of a peninsula sided by the muddy river that flowed in a horseshoe shape behind the Creek's good defensive position of formidable timbered barricade that stood higher than a man's head. Jackson ordered an assault after his Native Americans allies, mainly Cherokees but also anti-Redstick Creeks, swam the river to attack the Redsticks from the rear. Nearly 1,000 Redsticks were killed at bloody Horseshoe Bend, which was a decisive defeat that broke the back of the Redstick rebellion that never had a chance of succeeding. The towns and villages of the Creek country had been destroyed and crops burned to the ground by United States regulars and militiamen to remove substance for the tribe to ensure massive starvation. General Jackson became a great hero across the South and a national figure for having defeated the Creeks and he was celebrated across the United States. At last, the Creek War had come to an end.

The vindictive Treaty of Fort Jackson on August 9, 1814 was one of the greatest land grabs in American history, especially for the wealthy slave-owners and upper-class elites of the South because they benefitted the most. A staggering fourteen million prime acres, including the richest lands of Mississippi, Alabama, and Georgia, were officially stripped from the Creek people, including even the faithful Creek allies who fought beside Jackson, and the lands of all Indians living in the Southeast. In contrast, the Creek people had loved and respected the land according to the customs of their ancestors, while keeping it pristine and preserving it for hunting grounds. This land was possessed communally for the overall good and welfare of all tribal members in a complex society that was surprisingly egalitarianism and democratic.

But General Jackson also possessed a good military reason for taking the war deep into the Creek homeland, because of pressing strategic concerns and overall national security of the Southeast in the context of the raging War of 1812. He was determined to make sure that the Redsticks would never again utilize their British and Spanish allies in Spanish Florida, viewing his unauthorized march across the border and into Spanish Florida as a case of national defense in saving the Southeast and winning it for America. Indeed, and as mentioned, the Creek War was much more than stealing Indian lands, because the British and Spanish posed a serious threat to the Southeast, because the harbors along the Gulf of Mexico were used by the British Navy, especially Pensacola, Florida, making it possible for them to invade at any point along the lengthy southern coast. So, in the end, General Jackson made an invaluable contribution in the making of America and the winning of the Southeast by not only defeating the Creeks but also by eventually driving out of the British and the Spanish, whose presence threatened America.

Indeed, from the beginning, Jackson had especially desired to capture Pensacola to deny the British Navy access to the Gulf of Mexico, where they could strike inland with an invading army at any point along the southern coast. This was a great strategic advantage to the British who possessed the most powerful navy in the world. As part of the Chesapeake Campaign, the British Navy had raided along the eastern coast with impunity. The ever-opportunistic British even landed a task force in southern Maryland, and then they marched inland to burn down America's capital on August 27, 1814, after having reaped a decisive victory at the Battle of Bladensburg, Maryland, earlier in the day. So, the gulf obviously remained a threat to the security of America because of the strength of the British Navy and the possible landing of a British Army at any point.

As noted, no single man achieved more in winning the Southeast for America than General Jackson by spearheading the effort to secure Native American lands and Spanish Florida to end the British and Spanish threat, which was a serious one during the height of the War of 1812, when an ill-prepared and bumbling America was losing the war. He emerged as America's single shining light in the nation's darkest hour, when America was being embarrassed and humiliated by the powerful British during the War of 1812 by the extent of its ineptitude and inexperience. After the irrepressible Jackson had won the Creek War from 1813-1814 and as mentioned, the vast Creek lands of Alabama and Georgia were finally available to a perfect flood of whites, especially upper-class planters. Indeed, for the most part, these were only more prime acres for the rich who could afford to purchase large numbers of acres unlike poor men, like Crockett, who had fought the war. As like for most wars, the Creek War was a poor's man fight, but a rich man's war.

With the price of cotton on the rise to make the upper-class planter even wealthier from the highly lucrative combination of cotton gins and slaves, the Creek lands were shortly transformed into a great empire of cotton. These rich lands of Georgia and Alabama were turned into sprawling cotton plantations with large numbers of slaves, who worked the richest lands of the South from sunup to sundown under the bright sunshine. Indeed, it was members of the wealthy class who purchased most of the newly available Creek lands and their finest acres situated along the Flint and Chattahoochee Rivers of the Lower Creeks and the fertile lands of the Upper Creeks along the Alabama River and its tributaries like the Coosa and Tallapoosa, in Alabama. Unlike frontiersmen like Crockett without resources on the cash-short frontier, the wealthy planters purchased and settled in the most fertile bottomlands with the richest soils, while common soldiers of the lower class from the frontier missed the securing of the choicest acres. Of course, Crockett was one of these poor men, which was a price paid by a lower-class American frontiersman from the always impoverished frontier. As mentioned, the Creek lands were shortly transformed into a vast slave empire and Cotton Kingdom, thanks to the cruel process of Indian depopulation or what was basically ethnic cleansing, which then fueled even greater prosperity of the Southeast, especially among the planter class.

But now that the Creeks had been defeated and their fertile lands had been won for the creation of a vast empire of cotton and slaves, General Jackson was not finished because more hard work had to be done in the name of national security and protecting the people of the Southeast. He now looked even farther south to deal with the next threat that then needed to be eliminated, while the War of 1812 was still raging. Of course, and as noted, this was the British and Spanish presence in Florida, which he knew had to be ended at all costs. As a patriot, Crockett, like Jackson, saw and understood the strategic necessity of eliminating the foreign threat in the Southeast, which was the backyard of America.

But there was also another serious problem that had to be faced by Jackson and the United States Army: a breakaway tribe originally of the Creek Nation known as the Seminoles, who had fled farther south to escape Jackson's wrath and had settled in the pristine, untamed wilderness of southern Georgia and Spanish Florida. Some Seminoles had pushed as far south as Central Florida, which was a pristine and beautiful land of clear, blue lakes. From their hidden sanctuaries in Florida, the Seminole often raided north to strike the settlers and cotton planters in both southern Georgia and Florida. In his mind and like in vanquishing the Creeks, Jackson saw that the Seminoles were the next Native American people that needed to be eliminated to make the settlers safe and to remove another threat that could be exploited by the British and Spanish.

In consequence, it was Florida that now needed to be captured by General Jackson from the Spanish, because it represented the last obstacle to American security in the Southeast as the Spanish were allowing not only the

Seminole to reside in Florida, but also the former slaves who the Seminoles had liberated from plantations in their raids. Even more and as noted, many of the defeated Creeks had fled south into Florida and joined the Seminole, a new alliance that threatened the security of the settlers of the Southeast. This was no insignificant threat, because the British were encouraging the Native Americans (Creeks and Seminoles and their black allies) in Florida to strike the Americans and push them back farther north. Even more, both the British and Spanish, especially in Pensacola, the Spanish capital of West Florida, where the governor resided, were arming and supplying black powder to the warriors for the waging of war against the whites. Equally galling to General Jackson and whites was the fact that the blacks and Seminoles were natural allies and freely intermixed, becoming a new people and a new race that was fiercely anti-American and lifelong haters of slavery and white people in general, the Black Seminole. Raids of the Black Seminole resulted in the freeing of additional blacks held in bondage and they eagerly joined the war against the whites. All of these developments threatened the fragile security of the Southeast.

Although the Creek War was won and over, the War of 1812 continued unabated, and these new threats farther south had to be eliminated and General Jackson was determined to do just that. After his first term of Tennessee militia service had ended and after resting at home to regain his health and stamina from the long campaign in Creek territory, Crockett then enlisted in Major William Russell's

Tennessee Mounted Volunteers on September 28, 1814 on the eve of Jackson's new campaign in the Gulf of Mexico region to eliminate existing British, Spanish, Seminole, and black threats. Having long ago learned that the Spanish and British had been supplying Native Americans with guns and black powder, Jackson was determined to take Spanish West Florida, because it harbored Seminoles, former slaves, and defeated Creeks, who were supplied by British ships and the Spanish governor of West Florida.

Ironically, Crockett just narrowly missed the climax of General Jackson's invasion of Spanish Florida and his dramatic capture of Pensacola. But he successfully reached Jackson's army in the field on November 7, 1814 the day after General Jackson captured Pensacola from the Spanish governor and drove British warships, flying the Union Jack, out of the wide harbor. Crockett had arrived just in time to see the British ships sailing out of Pensacola harbor with white canvas sails bellowing in the warm breeze, which had been one of Jackson's longtime strategic goals that he knew was all-important in the war against the British. Indeed, this was an important victory reaped by General Jackson that came at a time when the United States was losing the War of 1812, having its capital of Washington, D.C., burned down on August 27, 1814. With his detachment of Major Russell's command, Crockett then scoured the swamps in Spanish Florida for escaped Redstick Creeks from the north, former slaves, and Seminoles until his discharge for service in 1815.

Having grown tired of the war when no satisfaction or glory could be reaped in trudging through the dreary swamps of Florida in chasing an elusive and cagy enemy that could not be caught, Crockett then returned home in February 1815, after having hired a friend to take his place in the ranks. In Crockett's own words later written half in jest and mockery about his undistinguished career as a soldier boy in the Florida wilderness: "This closed my career as a warrior and I am glad of it, for I like life now a heap better than I did then."

But it was not a completely wasted effort by volunteer Crockett, who had served as a scout and hunter who was known for his prowess with a flintlock rifle to acquire wild game for substance of the troops far from supply lines like earlier in the Creek War. It was a smart move that Crockett opted out of his period of service because campaigning in Spanish Florida ran the risks of becoming killed by the enemy or stricken with a deadly disease, while trudging through the dreary swamps and stinking, black waters of Florida. Crockett was fortunate not to have been stricken by a fatal disease like malaria, while other comrades were not so lucky. More good fortune was in store for Crockett in the future. He had gotten to know his future second wife, Elizabeth Patton, when a dying friend, who succumbed in 1813 during the Creek War, had asked that his personal belongings be returned to his wife, which was accomplished. By this time, Crockett was ready for a new wife when Polly Finley died in 1815 and Elizabeth was his prize, when he was a widow and his children needed a mother. They were about to be married.

General Jackson's hard-hitting ways for which he was famous proved decisive in the end. Pensacola was no longer a British and Spanish base after Jackson captured the strategic port town, which could have served as a British launching pad for invasion. Even more, Jackson begged the chief executive in Washington, D.C., to be allowed to capture all of Spanish Florida (Jackson said that he could "not rest" until Spanish Florida was taken) and take the war to Spanish Cuba by attacking Havana, if given a sailing ship by the government, which was the headquarters and source of Spanish troops in Florida. But President Madison knew that he was not ready for war with Spain, because he was already in a fight to the death with the British and it was not going well.

The War of 1812 concluded shortly after Jackson's great victory over the invading British at Chalmette on January 8, 1815, when he saved New Orleans from capture, after rushing his troops west from Florida to New Orleans just intime. Even more, Jackson had been ordered once again to Spanish Florida to "chastise a savage foe who combined with a lawless band of Negro brigands, have for some time past been carrying on a cruel and unprovoked war against the citizens of the United States." Jackson's aggression in West Florida in a second campaign in 1818 was the key catalyst that convinced Spain to cede Florida to the United States the following year. Incredibly, in short order, the general from Tennessee had broken the power of the Native

Americans, the British, and the Spanish in winning the Southeast, including Spanish Florida, for America.

Seemingly with his war days behind him forever and much to his relief after his return from inglorious duty in the maze of Florida swamps, Crockett embarked upon a political career when he won a seat in the United States House of Representatives as a Jackson supporter in 1827, 1829, and then again in 1833. But his political career was doomed in 1835, because he began speaking out and strongly opposing the popular President Jackson, especially his cruel Indian Removal Policy as inhuman. This was ample proof that Crockett was on the right side of history much to his everlasting credit.

Chapter II

"Land of Milk and Honey," Texas

Virginia-born Stephen Fuller Austin became known as the "Father of Texas," because his great dream of establishing a prosperous Anglo-Celtic colony on the fertile soil of Texas in the northeastern province of Mexico evolved into a sweet reality in the early 1820s. The ambitious Austin emphasized how: "My object and ambition was to succeed with the enterprise and lay a foundation for the fortune of thousands." Incredibly, the Spanish Government of New Spain had failed to develop its northeastern frontier of Texas, allowing some of the richest and most beautiful acres in North America, thanks partly to Indian threats of the southern Great Plains warriors like the Comanche, to languish and go to waste for decades.

Most of all, however, the Latino people of the New World possessed Mediterranean, Iberian Peninsula, and Roman roots that guaranteed that they were primarily an urban people and not a people who conquered and settled a wild frontier. In consequence, Mexico City had decided that they must secure hardy Anglo-Celtic settlers, who were known for their ability to defeat Native Americans across the frontiers of the United States, by offering them a liberal bounty of land to make this raw and untamed land productive at long last. But in the end, this ambitious strategic plan was destined to backfire. The Anglo-Celtics were mostly from the South and the antithesis of urban dwellers in almost every way. They and their ancestors had been a wandering and frontier people for generations, both in north Ireland and the United States, in always pushing farther west for better lands, which always meant that they long had to fight for possession of the land. They came to the right place in Texas, which was an unspoiled land just waiting to be developed by an industrious people, to create Stephen Full Austin's Colony of industrious settlers in a new land of plenty.

By far, the greatest lure for the Anglo-Celts who came to Texas was the vast amounts of land that could be secured for settling on this luxurious land from grants of land issued by the Republic of Mexico that had broken away from Spain in 1821. Then, after the Anglo-Celts of Texas rose up in revolt at Gonzales, Texas, in early October 1835, the new Texas republican government then also offered large bounties of land for volunteers who joined the Texas Army to fight for Texas in the revolution. This people's revolution had erupted from many grievances with Mexico City and then a hot skirmish that broken out between colonists and Mexican soldiers at Gonzales on October 2, 1835. The revolutionary government, known as the Texas General Council, had then requested volunteers, their old countrymen in the United States, to serve against Mexico with offers of land that were not only hard to resist but also almost incomprehensible to the average American, who hailed from the United States where free land was nonexistent: "We invite you to our country [actually that of Mexico]—We have land in abundance, and it shall be liberally bestowed on you [and] every volunteer in our cause shall not only justly but generously be rewarded."

A journalist presented a stirring appeal in a newspaper that was read far and wide across the United States: "Now in the moment for all young men, who want to create a name, and make a fortune, to bestir themselves. Go to Texas. Enroll yourself in the brave army of [Texas] . . . Because a country is before you. You will fight for a soil that will become your own [because Texas] is a territory equal to that of France—a soil far superior—a [warm] climate as healthy as any in the world . . . ." The liberal land bounty for a volunteer in the People's Army of Texas was originally 640 acres. But this amount significantly increased as the Texas Revolution continued, because of the urgent need to secure manpower from the United States. After March 2, 1836, the land bounty was raised by the government to an entire league of land, or 4,428 acres for a family of settlers. A single man without a family could gain 1,476 acres. This was an incredible and irresistible amount of land, especially for a poor or lower-class man from the United States.

Like for so many other Americans, the chance to gain thousands of prime acres was irresistible to forty-nine-year-old David Crockett, who was still a poor man despite having served as a Tennessee politician in the House of Representatives in the nation's capital on the Potomac River and having been a popular figure in the United States.

For generations, Crockett's family were mostly humble small farmers, including in the mountains of East Tennessee, where he had been born in a traditional log cabin at the edge of the Smoky Mountains on August 17, 1786 only three years after the end of the American Revolution. He possessed immigrant roots. The Crockett family had a French-Huguenot background, but the family had more recently lived in north Ireland, Ulster Province, before deciding to migrate to America. Since they lacked resources like most Irish immigrants, the family had settled on the cheapest lands on the frontier, including as squatters on Native American lands which was the cheapest means for immigrants of acquiring land.

By the mid-1830s, the Crockett family was still scratching out a meager living in northwest Tennessee in the Obrion River country. Crockett had experienced enough financial setbacks in life that he could never transition from a poor farmer and frontiersmen to a prosperous gentleman with many acres like the Southern planter elite—the American Dream at the time. Despite serving in the Creek War as only a common soldier and as mentioned, he failed to gain large amounts of Creek lands in one of the largest land grabs in American history. Like so many other Americans, Crockett sought a quick reversal and renewal of personal fortunes by settling in Texas and gaining large amount of land due to a settler, especially if he brought his family, from the United States. This was the magical formula for success and prosperity for an American without much land in the United States and whose future prospects were low. As mentioned, the key to success in American society was acquiring large amounts of land and this could be best and only be obtained in Texas. In consequence, Crockett was determined to pursue his dream of "staking out a very large ranch in Texas."

Nevertheless, the romantic myth has been created by Hollywood, the Disney Corporation, and historians that Crockett and his friends southwest rode to Texas in a burning rage to fight for Texas liberty and struggle for the freedom of the Anglo-Celts. This was simply not the case. Crockett's primary motivation for journeying to Texas had nothing to do with fighting or the Texas Revolution, but to start anew in life at age forty-nine in a bid to move higher in society and to improve the lives of himself and his wife and children. Crockett was determined and fueled by the hope of restoring his sagging personal and financial fortunes and even to begin a new political career in Texas, because he was so well-known and popular with Americans across the United States since he had been a favorite and popular figure in national politics.

By this time, Crockett was a bitter man. After his humiliating August 1835 defeat last summer in which he lost his Tennessee Congressional seat, he famously told his constituents: "You may all go the Hell & I will go to Texas." Clearly, Crockett was sick and tired of life in the United States, especially regarding politics in which the ever-popular President Andy Jackson had ensured his last defeat for Congress, and the frustration with not getting ahead in life in America, despite all of his futile efforts for decades.

As he revealed in a letter, Crockett had made up his mind to "go to the wilds of Texas," to "explore" Texas in preparation for starting anew in a bountiful land like his ancestors, who had left north Ireland and crossed the Atlantic in search of the American Dream. In the fall of 1835, Crockett and a small party of friends, including a nephew William Patton, mounted up on their horses and departed northwest Tennessee with high hopes for the future in starting new lives in Texas.

Like his ancestors who had migrated from Ulster Province, north Ireland, and crossed the Atlantic to start anew when in search of a brighter future, Crockett left home and family in Weakly County, Tennessee, on November 1, 1835 and rode for Texas for primarily economic reasons. Indeed, this was Crockett's last gamble and roll of the dice in attempting to get ahead in life. Going to Texas with friends and nephew William Patton was the "culmination of his efforts to get out of debt [because] he needed a big break and was looking for a homestead in a new country." But in the end, Crockett was destined to lose his great gamble in speculator fashion in the slaughter at the Alamo on the early morning of March 6, 1836. He would never again see his life or family again or Tennessee, after crossing the border and entering northeast Arkansas and heading southwest for Little Rock, which was the Arkansas capital in the state's center, before pushing farther southwest for Texas. Although he did not know it at the time, Crockett was riding straight into the storm of the Texas Revolution. But ironically to him, his timing could not have seemed better in the ultimate paradox, because of the lure of land.

Even more, the Texas revolutionaries had forced the last Mexican soldier out of Texas in December 1835 and it seemed as if the war was over. However, the ruthless president of Mexico, Antonio Lopez de Santa Anna, who modeled himself after his idol Napoleon Bonaparte, had other ideas and fancied himself as a mighty conqueror. In consequence, he was even now planning a resurgent offensive campaign to regain Texas for the Republic of Mexico. Of course, Crockett and his friends knew nothing about this ominous development, because they received no warnings whatsoever. Even the uniforms of Santa Anna's men resembled those of Napoleon's French soldiers and the dark-hued generalissimo wore his hair like Napoleon and collected Napoleonic memorabilia with considerable enthusiasm. Santa Anna would treat Anglo-Celtic rebels or even Mexican rebels, including Tejanos in Texas, who were against the central government with an utter ruthlessness that was genocidal, believing that they should all be exterminated to save Texas and keep it from being severed from the republic born of fiery revolution against the mother country.

Upon reaching northeast Texas after having been received like a hero and celebrity wherever he went during the long journey through Arkansas, Crockett's lofty expectations about Texas were far exceeded from anything that he had originally imagined. In utter amazement and hardly believing his eyes, he first explored the Red River country and the Red River Valley west of the Great Bend. He was amazed by what he saw around him, because nothing could have been more beautiful or pristine. Everywhere that Crockett looked were lush meadows, beautiful woodlands of virgin timber, and grassy prairies that stretched in every direction as far as the eye could see. Therefore and for ample good reason, Crockett described in a letter how the beautiful Red River country "the garden spot of the world." Crockett believed he was in a perfect hunter's heaven, as game was everywhere to be seen in a heavenly garden of delight that far exceeded all expectations.

Most of all, this was the place he hoped that he could gain his "league of land," consisting of thousands of prime acres of virgin land, for settling in Texas. In consequence, Crockett wrote his family a breathless letter: "I expect in all probability to settle on the Border of the Chactaw [Choctaw] Bro [Bayou] of Red River that I have no doubt is the richest country in the world." Clearly, Crockett's excited words could not have been more glowing to thrill his second wife, Elizabeth Patton Crockett who he had married in 1815 not long after his first wife Polly Finley had died, and family back in northwest Tennessee. Crockett was amazed by the sight of a virgin land of plenty.

A thoroughly delighted Crockett and his small party of Tennesseans departed the Red River frontier settlements on January 5, 1836 and rode south through more beautiful country, while continuing to explore a bountiful land that had been blessed by God. After reaching the small Anglo-

Celtic settlement of St. Augustine, east Texas and located just west of the Red River that served as the international border between Mexico and western Louisiana, he then wrote to his oldest daughter Margaret on January 9 about what was an early paradise: "What I have seen of Texas, it is the garden spot of the world, the best land & prospects to any man to come here; there is a world of country to settle, it is not required to pay down for your league of land; every man is entitled to a headright of 4438 A[cres] and they make the money to pay for it off the land."

Without worrying about the risks of settling in frontier Texas or the wrath of Native American raiders who struck when least expected, Crockett also emphasized to his family in the same letter how: "I am in great hopes of making a fortune for myself and family" in Texas "by way of large land-holdings." It all seemed like a fantastic dream that was almost too good to be true. Then, he continued exploring this unspoiled region of immense beauty and bounty that far exceeded anything in Weakley County and northwest Tennessee, while heading straight west and farther west from the Red River. Two days later after riding around thirty-five miles west from St. Augustine that had been recently established by Anglo-Celts in 1832, Crockett and company reached the largely Tejano town of Nacogdoches, Texas. Here, on January 14, he could hardly wait to sign the oath to the Texas Provisional Government and sign his enlistment papers to become a proud member of the Texas Volunteer Auxiliary Corps for a term of six months. Crockett believed that he had just made the shrewdest and smartest deal of his life without ever realizing that it was a true Faustian Bargain, which was a fatal one in the end for the forty-nine-year-old Tennessean, who was total enchanted by Texas.

Ironically, at this time because the revolutionary "Texians" were so confident and cocky after having expelled every Mexican soldier out of Texas in December 1835, Crockett and his men believed that they were shortly bound for Dr. James Grant's expedition in an attempt to capture the strategic commercial city on the Rio Grande River and located just west of its mouth in northeast Mexico in the lush Rio Grande Valley, Matamoros. But fate would shortly intervene when Crockett and his fellow volunteers would not be heading southeast to the port of Matamoros after all. Instead, they were ordered to ride southwest to San Antonio de Bexar and an old Spanish mission called the Alamo located in the Central Plains of Texas. All in all, the Alamo compound was in poor defensive shape and too large to properly defend by the small Anglo-Celtic garrison, if the Mexican Army ever suddenly returned to Texas, which the confident Anglo-Celts did not anticipate in their hubris. But, of course, Crockett was not aware of a host of strategic realities about Texas and the Texas Revolution, since he had only just arrived in this beautiful land called Texas.

As mentioned, Mexico, like the Spanish before them, had long viewed Texas as a problematic and troublesome province because its lack of settlers and prosperity, while Native Americans raids had long checked population growth. Hence, the Anglo-Celtic colonists had been introduced for the sole purpose of developing the land and making it a profitable appendage to Mexico City and the Republic of Mexico, which was far too authoritarian for Anglo-Celtic tastes and sensibilities. Even more, it was inevitable that Texas was coveted by settlers from the United States like Crockett, who wanted it for their own without any interference from Mexico: the genesis of open warfare and the inevitability of the Texas Revolution, which had always been only a matter of time.

Quite simply and in general, Mexican and Tejanos had been long unwilling to risk their lives far from the safety of the towns, especially Mexico City, because of fierce Apache and Commanche raiders who attacked with impunity and could not be stopped. Not so in the case of the Anglo-Celtics and frontiersmen like Crockett because they and their ancestors had long been familiar with daily life on dangerous frontiers far from assistance and support from the government for generations. In consequence, they knew how to tame a wild land and make it prosperous, which was in essence the fulfillment of the American Dream.

From the beginning, the Spanish and Mexicans had failed to settle in the remote north country so far north of Mexico City because they preferred to remain in Mexico City and large cities as they were an urban people by way of culture and heritage. The European heritage, or Spain in this case, of the Mexican people was also a factor. Known as Iberia since ancient times, Spain had been conquered by the Carthaginians from the great commercial state of

Carthage in north Africa and then the Romans, who were a Mediterranean people who loved city life. This distinct disinclination of the Latinos to settle in remote and isolated areas on a distant frontier had not significantly changed since the Spanish came to the New World, ensuring that most of the rural countryside—almost all of Texas—was uninhabited and unsettled in an undeveloped land, which had so astonished Crockett because of its unspoiled and pristine nature that was nothing less than breathtaking. Generation after generation, the Latinos had long positively avoided settling on the frontier, especially the northeastern frontier of Texas, because it was so remote and dangerous.

As noted, this situation was the antithesis of the Anglo-Celts who were a frontier people by instinct, ancestry, heritage, and distinct inclination for centuries. Drawn for centuries to frontier and remote areas like a magnet, they were exactly the kind of hardworking and industrious people who could finally tame not only the warlike Native Americans but also the wild land of Texas, which seemingly had been expressly made for them to fulfill their lofty dreams and ambitions that were nothing less than grandiose. To them, Texas was a golden idea and a vision that was in essence the American Dream.

Chapter III

Doomed at the Alamo

Crockett and his small party of mounted Tennesseans were doomed as soon as they were ordered to a new assignment at the largest Tejano town in Texas, San Antonio de Bexar, held by a small Anglo-Celtic garrison that was on its own on the isolated Texas southern frontier. Indeed, they were the southernmost defenders in central Texas to protect the bustling Anglo-Celtic settlements and extensive cotton plantations along the major rivers, which all flowed southeast into the Gulf of Mexico, in east Texas. After the journey southwest across a beautiful landscape of the open prairies of the vast Central Plain from the east Texas town of Nacogdoches, Crockett and his friends, who were all members of Captain William B. Harrison's Company of Mounted Volunteer, reached the Alamo on the 39th day of the calendar year, February 8, 1836. It was a Monday and one that Crockett never forgot. At the head of his "Tennessee Volunteers," he received royal treatment upon joining the small garrison that occupied both the town of San Antonio de Bexar and the Alamo located just to the east with the small San Antonio River in between. One hundred days had passed since Crockett and his friends had departed northwest Tennessee with high hopes about the future.

The Anglo-Celtic garrison, including some Tejanos, of under 200 men was far too small to hold both remote, widely-separated, and isolated positions—the town and the Alamo--amid the sprawling central plains. As a cruel fate would have it, Crockett's timing could not have been worse. From the time that he reached the Alamo, he now had less than 30 days to live. Crockett would have saved himself had he embarked on the Matamoros Expedition with the ambitious Dr. Grant who had been born in Scotland, but orders had suddenly changed that directed him and his comrades southwest to the place from where he would never return. Here, with the small Anglo-Celtic garrison and some Tejanos, Crockett considered himself nothing more than a "high private" of his "Tennessee Volunteers," although he was given special treatment because he was a former United States Congressman and a celebratory across America and in Texas, because it was inhabited by former United States citizens before they became proud "Texicans."

It is not known but Crockett might not have been in the cheeriest mood on February 8 upon reaching the Alamo. First, he felt little encouragement at the small size of the ragtag garrison located and exposed on the southern frontier of Texas, which was located far from the east Texas settlements and reinforcements. Then, Crockett had already suffered a severe political setback in having lost his Congressional seat that had caused him to depart the United States in the first place. As noted, the ambitious Tennessean also wanted to rejuvenate his political career in Texas in the process of beginning life anew to take advantage of a fresh start in life. Consequently, at the first opportunity for what he hoped would be a revival of his political that had come at Nacogdoches, he had made a bid to become a delegate at the upcoming Texas constitutional convention at Washington-on-the-Brazos in early March 1836. But Crockett had then learned to his dismay that he was ineligible by having just arrived on Texas soil and was not yet a permanent settler. Ironically, embarking either on the Matamoros Expedition or a political career would have saved Crockett's life. But a cruel fate and destiny had something else entirely different in store for David Crockett, because he would be stuck at the Alamo with a small garrison of citizen-soldiers.

And, of course, this was a calculated gamble by Crockett to gain his league of land because he was putting his life at stake. First and foremost, Crockett had to survive military service with all of its inherent risks. If he was killed, then he would never see the league of land that he so fondly dreamed about for himself and his family in a bright future in Texas. And Crockett's luck, as proven in the past life, was not conducive to winning gambles in life, especially large ones. Of course, here at the Tejano town of San Antonio de Bexar, Crockett had never been so far southwest in his entire life since he was now so far from his Weakly County home in northwest Tennessee. He knew nothing about the culture, values, and heritage of the Tejano people of San Antonio de Bexar, so he had to learn from scratch about the ways of this distinctive local people, the Tejanos, or

Mexicans born Texas. Even the Tejano children acted differently, not initially warming up the Anglo-Celts and their strange whiteness, while mainly staring in amazement at the strange-looking, white-faced interlopers from faraway with blank expressions, when they were smiled and waved at by a friendly garrison member.

San Antonio de Bexar was the largest town in south Texas and a bustling center of Tejano life, and large rancheros full of cattle dominated the surrounding countryside of grassy prairies. The ancestors of the upper-class elite of the town had come from the Canary Islands, owned by Spain and located just off the northwest coast of Africa. Clearly, Crockett was in an entirely alien environment that could not have been stranger to him. Ironically, Crockett was actually more familiar with the Creeks and their culture than the Tejanos. Texas had now become a bone of contention between two distinct people with entirely different cultures and backgrounds, including the old European rivalry of Catholicsm versus Protestantism.

In many ways and as mentioned, conflict between the Anglo-Celts and Mexico had been inevitable. First and foremost, the Spanish Government and then the Mexican Government, after 1821 when independence had been won, made a big mistake in allowing such large numbers of Anglo-Celts to settle in Texas and develop the land since it had been ignored and left idle by Mexico City for so long. After all, the Anglo-Celts were natural revolutionaries who resented authoritarian rules and high-handed dictates issued from Mexico City, including becoming good Catholics as they were already good Protestants. Leaders in Mexico City should have learned the bitter lessons in the loss of Spanish Florida, which had long been an early target of Anglo-Celtic revolutionaries and then was eventually lost to Spain when it was ceded to the United States in 1819. As noted, Crockett's old commander, Andrew Jackson, had played the largest role in the winning of Florida for America. And now he was sitting in the White House, while keeping a close eye on events in Texas, which he had long coveted for the Union. Instead of the Anglo-Celtic settlers becoming peaceful and faithful Catholics as naively expected in Mexico City, they had allowed the natural and tempestuous revolutionaries into their midst which was risky business— the genesis for the outbreak of the Texas Revolution in early October 1835.

All in all, Crockett found himself entirely out of his element in San Antonio de Bexar when stationed at a remote place that he knew nothing about, especially regarding the Tejano people. Unlike east Texas that was full of large cotton plantations and gangs of slaves like in the Deep South, Crockett found himself in a place where cotton culture had ended because San Antonio de Bexar was located on the Central Plains and it was located too far south and west in a much drier region that was mostly grasslands. As mentioned, San Antonio de Bexar was located on the Central Plains that was a world apart from east Texas. East Texas consisted of rich soil and ideal cotton country with plenty of rain and sunshine that was ideal for cotton cultivation: basically, the most westernmost extension of the fertile cotton belt that stretched across the South and even in Florida, the former Spanish possession where an earlier clash between different cultures and religions had resulted and Spain had lost to the Anglo-Celts. The fact that San Antonio de Bexar was a northern point of the largest centration of Tejano settlement also indicated that this region of broad, grassy plains was not cotton country.

Crockett had been assigned to defending a remote and isolated land that was at the point of two separate frontiers: the farthest point south and west of the Anglo-Celtic border to protest the east Texas settlements and a northern point of Mexican, or Tejano, settlement. In addition, this was the first time that Crockett had ever seen the southern portion of the Great Plains and it was a marvel to him. For a lifelong frontiersman who had spent most of his life in the dense eastern woodlands of America west of the Appalachian Mountains, the grasslands of the Central Plains could hardly have looked stranger to him, because there were no forests and only clumps of trees, mostly stately cottonwoods, could be seen and these were mostly located along creeks and the nearby San Antonio River, which flowed between the town and the Alamo.

While Crockett fondly dreamed of acquiring thousands of rich Texas acres as a reward for his service in the Texas Army, he failed to realize that the best and most fertile lands in Texas—the rich lands along the Colorado and Brazos Rivers that flowed southeast with broad deltas that entered the Gulf of Mexico—had already been claimed and settled by Anglo Celtic planters, who were mostly from the South, in the 1820s. Here, in east Texas, they had established a vast empire for slavery that served as the economic foundation of the Anglo-Celtic colony to make it prosperous, while slavery had been outlawed in Mexico: a forgotten reason for conflict that had also led to the Texas Revolution, because the Anglo-Celtic settlers feared Mexico's abolitionism would be applied to Texas, which would destroy the colony's thriving economy based on cotton cultivation. Much to Crockett's lament and as mentioned, these prized acres of east Texas had already been grabbed by wealthy planters, who had earlier migrated across the Mississippi from the South with plenty of plantation experience, money, and slaves to do all the work.

In consequence and as fate would have it, Crockett had already missed out on the chance of acquiring the best and most fertile cotton lands, which was the farthest westward extension of the cotton belt of the Deep South that stopped with the rich lands of east Texas. This was much like after the Creek War, because he had failed to gain of large portion of any of the rich Creek lands, especially along the rivers, in today's Alabama, Mississippi, and Georgia that became part of the fertile cotton belt of the Deep South. As a poor man, Crockett simply did not have the money to purchase large numbers of virgin acres. And for whatever reason, he failed to gain substantial Creek lands for his service in the Creek War of 1813-1814. All in all, this was the situation that had caused him to journey to Texas in the first place with plans of relocating his family from the overused, eroded lands of northwest Tennessee to a virgin land of endless promise and opportunities. Like his ancestors from north Ireland, it was time to move on and farther away from Tennessee to find his American Dream that now only existed far-away in Texas.

While Crockett envisioned how he would one day own a large Southern-like plantation in Texas to join the upper-class elite and the elevated lifestyle of a proper gentleman which was the obtaining of the American Dream that dominated the South, this was now an impossible dream for him that was unknown to him, because his great dream had already passed him by in what was the former Tennessee Congressman's last illusion and dream. From beginning to end, this was a great American Dream that was destined to be the most elusive one in his entire life. Crockett was about to pay a high price for having been a poor man for his entire life and having missed out in the game of gaining his American Dream in the past now that he was nearly age fifty. Instead of the enduring popular myth, thanks to Hollywood, imaginative scriptwriters, and traditional historians that have emphasized Crockett was most of all motivated by his eagerness of fight against the Mexicans for republican government, patriotism, righteous sentiments, and heady enlightenment idealism against the tyranny of a dictatorship that resided in Mexico City and whose army now was marching northward San Antonio de Bexar, this was simply not the case. Going to Texas and joining the Texas Army was merely a means to an end for Crockett and it was all about economics.

In truth and now that he had his long-elusive American, or Texas, Dream within his grasp or so it seemed, Crockett hoped that there would be no more fighting, after the last occupying Mexican soldier had been driven out of Texas, which occurred not long after the Anglo-Celtic rebels captured Mexican held-San Antonio de Bexar and the Mexican-held Alamo in December 1835. Crockett hoped that he could gain his large number of Texas acres—more than 4,000 that were entitled to him if he settled his family--without risking his life and without a shot fired in anger during his six-month term of service in the Texas revolutionary army, after which he would gain his own American Dream on Texas soil. This rosy scenario seemed most likely, if not inevitable, to Crockett in the late winter of 1836. So, it seemed as if Crockett had arrived in Texas at the ideal time, especially if there would be no more fighting if Mexican soldiers remained out of Texas. Quite simply, he could gain his thousands of precious Texas acres by not firing a shot in anger or fighting against a single Mexican soldier, if everything stayed quiet and peaceful in Texas.

Indeed, as this time, the Anglo-Celts, whose confidence had never been higher, across Texas believed that President Santa Anna would never dare to march north from deep in Mexico with an army only to be once again defeated by the rustic revolutionaries on Texas soil. This was a common concept in the xenophobic and racist minds of whites who viewed Mexicans, because of their darker skins that reflected an Aztec heritage, as not only the same as Native Americans but also black slaves, who were viewed as subhuman. Therefore, if Santa Anna dared to march north into Texas then he would be easily defeated just like the Indians of the Creek War of 1813-1814, according to the common consensus at the time. To Crockett, consequently, it had seemed that enlisting and serving in the Texas Army was practically risk-free, and that he could gain all of those golden Texas acres without ever risking his life or firing a shot in anger, if there was no more fighting.

But a cruel fate and destiny was already set in place against Crockett and his heady visions and optimism for the future now that he had all but gained his ever-elusive American Dream in a new bountiful and beautiful land of plenty at age forty-nine. Again, to Crockett, such a virgin and pristine land seemed almost unbelievable and too good to be true. If all worked out according to plan and with his heady vision that was now well within his reach at this time, then Crockett would have accomplished and achieved far more than his father and grandfather regarding moving up higher in American society and life. Crockett could become a wealthy man from the considerable profits of fields of cotton grown on a working plantation of more than 4,000 acres, which was an estate unimaginable to any of his ancestors or to him before he rode to Texas. In fact, the first Crockett family members had departed Ireland because almost all of the land of the Emerald Isle was owned by the wealthy English and Anglo-Irish elites, who had squeezed out the lower and middle-class Irish, who were exploited as renters on the lands of the vast estates owned by the wealthy elite, which had forced them to migrate to America.

However and as noted, Crockett had already missed out on achieving the American Dream both in the United States and Texas, because all of the best acres, especially along the creeks and rivers, had already been purchased and settled, especially in east Texas. He had already missed out in the giant land grab of the taking of millions of acres of Creek lands after the Creek War and now had to risk his life in obtaining a large portion of land in Texas that he was destined to never receive, because Santa Anna was determined to regain Texas for Mexico forever more. In much the same way, Crockett now found himself in the middle of a people's revolution on the southwest frontier for the express purpose of obtaining large numbers of Texas acres that would be a reward for his six-month service as a volunteer in the Texas Army if he served to August 1836, while he was only hoping for the best in the future and not desiring to fight armies from Mexico.

Surprise Attack in the Blackness of the Night

In fact, time was now already rapidly running out for David Crockett, former Tennessee Congressman, by the time that he reached the Alamo on February 8. General Santa Anna, the president of Mexico, was leading a mighty army north for San Antonio de Bexar, where he knew from spies that only a small garrison of Anglo-Celts had gathered to defend the strategic town on the southern frontier of Texas. On February 12, thousands of troops of Santa Anna's Army crossed the Rio Grande River and headed straight north for San Antonio de Bexar. At all costs, Santa Anna was determined to regain the honor lost to Mexico when the last Mexican soldier had evacuated San Antonio de Bexar, after it was surrendered to the Anglo-Celts and then they were allowed to return to Mexico in shame and humiliation in December 1835. The resurgent Mexicans were now coming back to destroy the ragtag, motley band of gringo rebels stationed San Antonio de Bexar, which was the largest town in Texas, and take back the Tejano town on the Central Plains for the Republic of Mexico in the first stage of eliminating rebels and the curse of rebellion in Texas.

Crockett and other members of the small garrison, under the command of young South Carolinian William Barret Travis, had no idea that an entire Mexican Army with revenge chiefly on its agenda was rapidly headed their way in overwhelming numbers partly because the accurate reports of Tejano scouts were dismissed. As cleverly planned, Santa Anna caught the San Antonio garrison completely by surprise by his sudden arrival on February 23. On the double, the Anglo-Celts barely escaped into the Alamo on the other side, or east, of the San Antonio River. But now this old Spanish mission that had once Christianized large numbers of local Native Americans was a certain deathtrap for the Anglo-Celts.

In desperation, Travis sent out appeals by courier for reinforcements, but it was too little, too late. However, a courageous band of 32 mounted volunteers of the Gonzales Ranger Company from the small town of Gonzales, where the war began in early October 1835, slipped through Mexican lines and entered the Alamo around 3:00 am on March 1. But, of course, this was not enough to prevent the inevitable, which would be a slaughter of all garrison members. Worthy of Napoleon in a tactical sense, Santa Anna had developed a masterful, if not brilliant, attack plan that was destined to catch the garrison by surprise in the early morning darkness of March 6, 1836.

Because there were no survivors of Santa Anna's attack among garrison members on the early morning of March 6, no one knows how Crockett died, when he was stationed in defending the wooden palisade near the Alamo chapel with other member of Captain Harrison's company of volunteers, including the Tennesseans. But that fact is simply not important at all in the end. Nevertheless, generations of traditional American writers, historians, and filmmakers have created the most heroic death possible for Crockett in keeping with core concepts of American heroism, patriotism, and mythmaking to the point of transforming him into some kind of American Superhero, while Mexicans accounts have bestowed quite the opposite portrayal. Mexican accounts have revealed that Crockett surrendered and then was executed, but this cannot be confirmed, because of the unreliability of some of these accounts, especially those with a proper providence. Of course, the real truth about Crockett's death at the Alamo is somewhere in the middle in a shade of gray rather than black or white created by opposing agendas, including for political, racial, and cultural reasons.

But I would like to believe and think that David Crockett's demise at the Alamo was comparable to how it has been portrayed on the cover of this current book. For a much more detailed and comprehensive book about the Alamo, Crockett, and the dynamics of the Texas Revolution, please see my 2010 book *Exodus from the Alamo, The Anatomy of the Last Stand Myth*, which broke more new ground than any book about the Alamo, both before and since.

Epilogue

The truthful story of the life of David Crockett looks nothing at all like what has been long presented for generations to the American people for a variety of reasons, including political factors.

In the Cold War during the great 40-year showdown between the democracies of the West and the Communism of the Soviet Union, the United States needed an authentic American hero to be celebrated and idolized by the American people for generations.

Ironically, it was a private corporation, Disney, that chose "Davy" Crockett (a decision of Walt Disney himself) to teach Americans about heroism and the virtues of republican government.

In the process, Crockett's life was greatly embellished and glorified until it was unrecognizable with the historical facts, which told a much different story.

The glorification of the highly marketable Crockett image disguised the reality that Crockett's life was one dominated by personal defeat and setbacks: the antithesis of what had been long portrayed to the American public in much exaggerated form.

From beginning to end, he was a poor frontiersman who struggled in vain his entire life to obtain his American Dream and never succeeded, despite his best efforts.

Crockett was only in Texas in a last-ditch bid to obtain the ever-elusive American Dream, but all of Crockett's heady visions and ambitions came to an ugly and bloody end on the early morning of March 6, 1836 at the Alamo, when Santa Anna unleashed his surprise attack and slaughtered very garrison member.

Bibliography

Crockett, David, *A Narrative of the Life of David Crockett of the State of Tennessee*, (Lincoln: Bison Books, 1981).

Cusick, James G., and Johnson, Sherry, editors, *Andrew Jackson in Florida, 1814-1821, Forging His Legacy*, (Cocoa: The Florida Historical Society Press, 2016).

Halbert, Henry Sale and Dale, Timothy Horton, *The Creek War of 1813-1814*, (Whitefish: Kessinger Press, 2009).

Kly, Y. N., editor, *The Invisible War, African American Anti-Slavery Resistance from the Stono Revolt through the Seminole War*, (Atlanta: Clarity Press, 2006).

Martin, Joel W., *Sacred Revolt, The Muskogee's Struggle for a New World*, (Boston: Beacon Press, 1991).

Porter, Kenneth W., *The Black Seminole, History of a Freedom-Seeking People*, (Gainesville: University of Florida Press, 2013).

Scheina, Robert L., *Santa Anna: A Curse upon Mexico*, (Washington, D.C.: Potomac Books, 2002).

Tucker, Phillip Thomas, *Exodus from the Alamo: The Anatomy of the Last Stand Myth*, (Philadelphia: Casemate Publishers, 2010).

Wallis, Michael, *David Crockett: The Lion of the West*, (New York: W.W.W. Norton and Company, 2012).

Zinn, Howard, *A People's History of the United States*, (New York: Harper, 1995).

About the Author

VISIT HIS AUTHOR PAGE ON AMAZON
PHILLIP THOMAS TUCKER

OR VISIT THE AUTHOR'S WEBSITE
https://www.phillipthomastuckerphd.com/

PHILLIP THOMAS TUCKER, Ph.D., has won recognition as a national award-winning historian and America's most prolific groundbreaking "New Look" historian in multiple fields of history. He has authored more than 130 books in many fields of history, while gaining an international reputation as "the Stephen King of History." Best known for presenting fresh perspectives and original ideas to demythologize traditional history long outdated, Tucker has authored more than 200 works, both scholarly books and articles, of history that have long overturned outdated books of traditional history.

The winner of prestigious national awards and well-known as "a creative, innovative thinker, who has a gift for conceiving and outlining original works in serious history," he has emerged as America's most iconoclastic and prolific historian in the 21st Century. Tucker's groundbreaking history books have been widely praised on both sides of the Atlantic from the *New York Times* to the *London Times*. A fellow Ph.D. in history and professional historian emphasized how "Tucker is one of the most innovative, hardest working, and diligently productive" historians in America.

Tucker has become one of America's top historians in the field of Revolutionary War history, authoring groundbreaking books like GEORGE WASHINGTON'S SURPRISE ATTACK; BROTHERS OF LIBERTY; SAVING WASHINGTON'S ARMY; ALEXANDER HAMILTON'S REVOLUTION; HOW THE IRISH WON THE AMERICAN REVOLUTION; KINGS MOUNTAIN; ALEXANDER HAMITON AND THE BATTLE OF YORKTOWN; and others.

Presenting vibrant historical narratives and cutting-edge history distinguished by new perspectives and insights, the author has written more than 110 highly original books of unique distinction. Tucker's RANGER RAID has presented a close look at the most audacious and daring raid in the annals of American military history—the attack of Major Robert Rogers and his Rangers on St. Francis, while breaking much new ground in the field. This 2021 book has broadened the author's range of important books that have focused on fascinating subjects from the French and Indian War to the Second World War.

He also has completed books of international interest in the field of Women's history, including MULAN AND THE MODERN CONTROVERSY, THE UNCONQUERABLE SPIRIT OF A YOUNG AND COURAGEOUS CHINESE WOMAN; THE TRUNG

SISTERS; Four Volume of the HARRIETT TUBMAN SERIES; LAKSHMI BAI; SOLITUDE OF GUADELOUPE; GRAN TOYA (Volume I of a four-volume HAITIAN REVOLUTIONARY WOMEN SERIES), etc. He has also authored groundbreaking works in Women's history, with JOSEPHINE BAKER; MARY EDMONIA LEWIS; FEMALE APACHE WARRIOR AND SHAMAN OF HER PEOPLE, LITTLE SISTER LOZEN; CAVALRY CAPTAIN NADEZHDA DUROVA; CHARLOTTE L. FORTEN'S BROKEN HEART; OLYMPE DE GOUGES, etc.

More than 25 of Tucker's books have been written about the distinguished legacies of black heroes and heroines, including a new book about the forgotten mother of the Civil Rights Movement, CLAUDETTE COLVIN; four volumes devoted to heroine Harriet Tubman; four books about the remarkable life of female Buffalo Soldier CATHY WILLIAMS; four volumes devoted to the most famous black regiment (the 54th Massachusetts) of the Civil War; etc. He has written more than a dozen books about unforgettable black women to reveal their rich contributions and sacrifice in America's story and Caribbean history.

Very few historians have so expertly combined academic and popular history to vividly recreate the past from mere scraps of historical evidence to continuously break new ground and present fresh perspectives, while shattering historical myths and providing distinctive "New Look" perspectives to illuminate historical narratives than Tucker. Unlike traditionally told historical narratives from only one side or perspective, the author has allowed readers to view the most ignored and forgotten side of history, especially black history and women's history, to bestow a more balanced and honest perspective to the historical record.

First and foremost, Tucker's books are stores about people of all races and classes who were caught in monumental historical events beyond their control and power to escape, while presenting hard-hitting and brutally realistic and honest narratives. As much as possible, the author tells these stores through the eyes and experiences of the participants.

One of the author's most recent books has been devoted to the incredible saga of teenage Claudette Colvin, which is a heroic story of defiance and protest in the face of impossible odds. Tucker's CLAUDETTE COLVIN, FORGOTTEN MOTHER OF THE CIVIL RIGHTS MOVEMENT is an especially timely and important work for all Americans today. Significantly, Dr. Tucker has been the most prolific and groundbreaking author in black history in the last 50 years, including the books CUSTER'S FORGOTTEN BLACK SOULMATE, NAT TURNER'S HOLY WAR AGAINST SLAVERY, FATHER OF THE TUSKEGEE AIRMEN, JOHN C. ROBINSON, DAVID FAGEN (2 volumes); CHARLOTTE L. FORTEN'S BROKEN HEART; JOSEPHINE BAKER; MARY EDMONIA LEWIS, and four volumes about female Buffalo Soldier CATHY WILLIAMS.

Dr. Tucker's books are distinguished by a unique fusion of enlightenment with groundbreaking history and fresh perspectives to reveal important historical narratives that have been long-ignored and forgotten in the traditional narrative. Tucker earned national recognition in winning one of America's most prestigious national awards for the best non-fiction book in Southern history in 1993. Dr. Tucker also enjoyed a distinguished career as a Department of Defense historian, primarily in Washington, D.C., for more than two decades, including duty in working on the personal staff of the Chief of the United Sates Air Force at the Pentagon, Washington, D.C.

This prolific author has been long known for innovative and creative thinking outside the box to present different and fresh views to solve historical mysteries and overturn traditional historical viewpoints. Tucker's iconoclastic books are widely-known to be as hard-hitting as they are groundbreaking, including CUSTER AT GETTYSBURG, A NEW LOOK AT GEORGE ARMSTRONG CUSTER VERSUS JEB STUART IN THE BATTLE'S CLIMACTIC CAVALRY CHARGES: the most important Civil War book of corrective Gettysburg history released in the 21st Century. The History Book Club lavishly praised this groundbreaking book—"a book combining two popular subjects [and] author and historian Phillip Thomas Tucker recounts the story of Custer at Gettysburg with verve."

Dr. Tucker's books have been featured by the History Book Club for more than three decades. He has earned the rare distinction as the only historian in the long history of the History Book Club whose important books have been featured for three consecutive decades.

Fellow professional historians have long recognized Dr. Tucker's "gift for conceiving and outlining original works in serious history [which is] his longest suit as a professional historian," in the words of one distinguished academic historian and fellow Ph.D. in the field of history. Even more, America's most prolific author in history in the twenty-first century has achieved recognition at "the most innovative, hardest working, and diligently productive [historian] of his generation."

Tucker's well-researched, scholarly books have presented cutting edge "New Look" history that have provided fresh views about the nation's most important turning point moments in American history. A 2020 History Book Club and Military Book Club Selection like six of the author's other books, Tucker's CUSTER AT GETTYSBURG has been acclaimed by leading experts as thoughtfully penetrating, while illuminating the most forgotten chapter of Gettysburg history. This groundbreaking book has overturned the outdated obsolete books by emphasizing the importance of the crucial cavalry role at Gettysburg on July 3, 1863. Representing the author's 7th Gettysburg book in his well-known myth busting tradition, CUSTER AT GETTYSBURG has presented a corrective analysis to explain the most neglected reason for decisive Union victory at Gettysburg, when Custer and his Michigan men saved the day.

CUSTER AT GETTYSBURG, the most scholarly book ever written about this forgotten turning point in Civil War and American history, has overturned generations of outdated Gettysburg historiography, while once again revealing the author's long-time and well-known penchant for writing groundbreaking history. The History Book Club editor wrote how this important book tells the story "Where the legend of Custer was born," and how "Custer's true rise to prominence began on the battlefield of Gettysburg [and Tucker] shows how the Custer legend was born [in] the war's most famous battle, an eye-opening new perspective on Gettysburg's overlooked cavalry battle" to reconfirm the author's widespread reputation as America's leading "New Look" historian.

By presenting cutting edge history, Dr. Tucker's many books have turned traditional historical narrative upside down to present fresh views and perspectives from meticulous research, while rewriting the romanticized, obsolete history that has been incorrectly presented to us by old school traditionalists. In consequence, Tucker has emerged as America's most groundbreaking and prolific historian, presenting corrective history of importance in a flood of groundbreaking books. This award-winning writer has written more than 5 million words in more than 100 books of unique distinction in a wide range of highly-specialized fields of history, while maintaining a high quality output of corrective history over a lengthy period of time during two different centuries: an accomplishment not achieved by any American historian during the last half century.

For decades, Dr. Tucker has bestowed recognition to forgotten women, black and white, of distinction and other ignored players in America's story to leave a lasting literary achievement in multiple fields of history. No American historian has broken more new ground in so many books of historical significance in so many diverse fields of history than this prolific author. While chronicling important lives in colorful narratives that are educational, Tucker has written uniquely human and cutting-edge history in truly iconoclastic books that enlighten and inspire readers.

The author earned a Ph.D. in American History at a prestigious Jesuit institution, St. Louis University, where he was "part of a tradition of academic excellence." Tucker then served his country for more than two decades at military bases across the United States as a Department of Defense civilian historian, including working at the Pentagon in Washington, D.C.

As noted, Tucker has often illuminated major turning point moments in American history, including his highly acclaimed PICKETT'S CHARGE, A NEW LOOK AT GETTYSBURG'S FINAL ATTACK (distributed by Simon and Schuster). This groundbreaking book was lavishly praised by Yale graduate Thomas E. Ricks, one of America's most distinguished historians, in his NEW YORK TIMES REVIEW (11/10/2016), "Thomas Ricks on the Season's Military History." Please see this NEW YORK TIMES review at:

https://www.nytimes.com/2016/11/13/books/review/new-military-history-books.html

Gettysburg expert and scholar, Bradley M. Gottfried, Ph.D., former College of Southern Maryland president, emphasized how Tucker's PICKETT'S CHARGE is "easily the best book on the topic."

The author's CUSTER AT GETTYSBURG has set the historical record straight after more than a century and a half, while revealing a forgotten turning point moment in American history: George Armstrong Custer's vital role in helping to win the Battle of Gettysburg on July 3, 1863. CUSTER AT GETTYSBURG is even a more groundbreaking and important work than Tucker's PICKETT'S CHARGE. This scholarly work has overturned the many outdated Gettysburg books by traditional authors still clinging to outdated orthodoxy and tradition. Tucker has completed another important Custer book entitled, WHY CUSTER WAS NEVER WARNED to reveal the forgotten true story about the Battle of the Little Bighorn and much like his groundbreaking DEATH AT THE LITTLE BIGHORN.

During the past decades, no historian today has broken more new ground in the Gettysburg field than Dr. Tucker, including his recent AMERICA'S BLOODY HILL OF DESTINY. Dr. Tucker has authored seven unique and important Gettysburg books with "New Look" perspectives and a distinctive Cattonesque narrative style and energetic style of writing, while providing a wealth of new ideas, fresh views, and insightful perspectives. He has overturned generations of conventional wisdom and outdated Gettysburg history in groundbreaking books like BARKSDALE'S CHARGE, THE IRISH AT GETTYSBURG, STORMING LITTLE ROUND TOP, GETTYSBURG'S MOST HELLISH BATTLEGROUND, etc.

Tucker has become the most prolific "New Look" scholar in Gettysburg, blacks, Irish, and women's studies in the 21st Century. He has presented many unique aspects of history—military, social, political, racial—in a new and fresh way, including his recent books of the new Harriet Tubman Series of four volumes. As mentioned, Tucker's books have been of an extremely groundbreaking nature never before achieved by a single author. For instance, one expert emphasized about the author's DEATH AT THE LITTLE BIGHORN how: "no one has made a stronger case for what really happened than Phillip Thomas Tucker in this compelling and convincing narration."

Even more, the author's books are distinguished by a vivid, lively descriptive style of writing unlike the dry, textbook style so common in history books. Tucker has long focused on some of America's best human interest stories and historical vignettes. Describing characters and events in great detail, the author's unique narrative style, often poetic, in overall vivid descriptiveness, has allowed readers to be transported back in time to stirring moments in history. By bringing forgotten men and women vividly back to life, Tucker has written dozens and dozens books of rare distinction that are extremely enlightening and educational. A narrative and descriptive historian with a Ph.D. who has successfully merged these dual strengths in a rare combination not often seen in any writer, Tucker has allowed readers to gain an intimate feel for history like few other authors today. Most important, Dr. Tucker has become America's most prolific ground-breaking historian in many fields of history: an unprecedented achievement to date.

An innovative, out-of-the-box thinker recognized on both sides of the Atlantic, Tucker has authored highly original "New Look" narratives to reveal new insights and perspectives to prove that the best history definitely goes against the grain and tradition. Insightful and thoughtful Daniel N. White emphasized a fundamental truth in his 9/20/2011 review of the author's myth-busting EXODUS FROM THE ALAMO: "Finally, The Truth About the Alamo."

Tucker earned three history degrees from prestigious universities, including a Ph.D. in American history from St. Louis University in 1990, while gaining a 4.00 GPA. In books distinguished by their broad human appeal and fresh interpretations, the author has most often untangled historical half-truths to present more accurate history by more deeply exploring the deep complexities of the human experience on multiple levels, such as the lives of Buffalo Soldiers David Fagen and Cathy Williams.

Significantly, this myth-busting historian has also illuminated some of the most climactic and crescendo moments in American history from the American Revolution to the Second World War, while establishing new literary benchmarks in Women's, African American,

Caribbean, American Revolutionary War, Tuskegee, Civil War, Abolition, Buffalo Soldier, Irish, Little Bighorn, Pirate, Aviation, Western, Spanish-American War, Gettysburg, and Southern history.

As noted, Tucker's iconoclastic books have especially bestowed greater recognition to long-ignored African American men and women. The author has emerged as one of the most important historians in the field of African American history like in other fields of history in the last century. The author's groundbreaking series (54th MASSACHUSETTS GLORY SERIES of four volumes) of books have celebrated the heroics of the North's first black regiment during the Civil War: the first series of books ever devoted to this remarkable black regiment that brought forth a new birth of freedom to America.

Significantly, Dr. Tucker's books about black history have also focused on bringing about greater social awareness to Americans, both black and white, today, about black heroes and heroines who have been long overlooked and forgotten. In highly original "New Look" narratives, the author has promoted the heroics of brave African American men, aviator pioneer John C. Robinson, and black women from the American Revolution to the Second World War, including multiple series of important and groundbreaking books.

As noted, Tucker's "New Look" books have focused on the heavily Buffalo Soldier experience (2 volumes about David Fagen and 4 volumes about Harriet Tubman) and Jamaica's national heroine Nanny and revolutionary women of Haiti. Tucker's first book (2002) about the remarkable life of female Buffalo Soldier Cathy Williams was praised by Library Journal: "A unique story of gender and race . . . that reaches across categories, from American,

African American, and military history to Western and Women's history."

Like his other revealing books in African American history, Tucker has accomplished a comparable significant literary feat in the fascinating field of Irish history like in black history. The author has written about the forgotten Irish contributions in the Civil War, Texas Revolution, and westward expansion, including: HOW THE IRISH WON THE AMERICAN REVOLUTION; THE IRISH AT GETTYSBURG; GOD HELP THE IRISH! HISTORY OF THE IRISH BRIGADE, and other noteworthy books, including award winners.

Talented historian and scholar Perry D. Jamieson, Ph.D., emphasized how: "What separates [Tucker] from many other historians is that he is an innovative 'idea person.' I have known very few historians who can match his ability to conceive a topic, develop a fresh approach to it, and write about it at length."

In correcting the historical record in his national award-winners, Best Sellers, and History and Military Book Club Main Selections, Tucker has overturned America's oldest prevailing myths and stereotypes, especially racial, in multiple fields of history. From the beginning, a historian's greatest gift has been to present the familiar in new ways and this achievement has become Dr. Tucker's expertise and specialty.

Most of all, Tucker's books have reinterpreted history around the world to provide a good many fresh and new perspectives, allowing a new generation of readers to rediscover America's fascinating past through a sharper lens and more intensified focus, especially in terms of race and gender. One professor emphasized Tucker's educational contributions that have brought history alive like few other historians: "thousands of tourists may now be exposed to what has been washed out by narratives" for generations. By conceiving original history in multiple fields, he has emerged today as America's leading corrective historian and deconstructionist of outdated history. Described as a "once in a generation historian," Tucker has authored ground-breaking "New Look" books that present unique perspectives for the twenty-first century, while overturning the traditional historical narrative. One revered historian concluded: "Dr. Tucker is one of the two or three best 'idea persons' that I've met during my nearly twenty years as a professional military historian." By digging deeper to solve history's mysteries and to unravel its many riddles, Tucker has dismantled some of the most sacred cows in American history.

Throughout his long career, Dr. Tucker has always taken the road least traveled by historians by focusing on unique "New Look" perspectives in vivid historical narratives that have been groundbreaking. Tucker has praised the American fighting man, while simultaneously promoting greater social awareness. Struggles against the odds and convention by forgotten underdog players have been a primary theme of Tucker's many biographies, especially those about African American women. One professor praised this award-winning author educated at St. Louis University "for making the study of mankind a real narrative."

The author's many books are distinguished by their overall humanity to reveal history's most intimate and personal side, which has been too often ignored by other historians. In one astute reviewer's words: "Most history in printed form has very little, if any humanity [but the author's books] made a profound impact on me, due not only to razor-sharp depictions of strategy and its execution, but something that was revealed with astonishing empathy: the Truth."

Tucker's books have most often gone against the grain of the traditional consensus and standard narrative to present some of the most fascinating chapters of America's most hidden history by focusing on revealing long-silenced voices and stories long forgotten. One historian emphasized that in Tucker's DEATH AT THE LITTLE BIGHORN: "Custer's Last movements and decisions have been argued about since 1876, but, in my mind, no one has made a stronger case for what really happened than Phillip Thomas Tucker in this compelling and convincing narration."

PICKETT'S CHARGE (Main Selection of the History Book Club) also garnered considerable praise from leading experts across America. One reviewer emphasized how the author "Replaces 150 years of uninterrogated mythology with meticulously research history to give us a new and long-overdue understanding" of this key turning point moment in American history.

Tucker's "New Look" 2010 EXODUS FROM THE ALAMO, THE ANATOMY OF THE LAST STAND MYTH (a History Book Club Selection sold at the Alamo for years and to this day) has overturned generations of mythical Texas history, which has been grossly distorted for nearly two centuries. A *Library Journal* review emphasized that "Tucker provides long-overdue corrections to the Alamo story unknown to most readers." Another reviewer concluded: "I commend Phillip Thomas Tucker for uncovering the ugly truth" about Texas and its dark history, especially when it came to slavery and race relations. In mid-August 2011, *The Times* and *Daily Mail* of London,

England, featured complimentary lead stories that praised "Exodus from the Alamo."

FAKE AMAZON 1-Star and 2-Star ATTACK REVIEWS: One contributor to a Civil War blog revealed the motivation behind an organized campaign of rivals who have engaged in years of posting fake 1-star Amazon reviews for the author's books in an organized smear campaign: "Did you pan it on Amazon? . . . stop Tucker before he writes again." Only one or two cyber cowards (false and fake attack reviews that are excessively editor obsessive since they obviously came from a rival editor and publisher) have been behind the posting of more than 250 fake 1-star Amazon reviews against the author's works for more than a decade. One publisher, whose editors of Tucker's books have been repeatedly smeared by them with their lies, concluded how "they are simply scum."

EXODUS FROM THE ALAMO Reviews by Leading Experts:
—"The research is hard to argue against [and] is pretty straight forward. Read all of it with an open mind [and] You will surprise yourself," *Kepler's Military History.*
—"Tucker provides long-overdue corrections to the Alamo story unknown to most readers," *Library Journal.*
—"Tucker has written a remarkable account of one of America's pivotal military actions," *Military Heritage Magazine.*
—"Tucker's bold assessment is undeniably true," *City Book Review.*
—"My, My, My, we now have a truthful book about the Alamo [by the] complete demolition of the Texas founding myth done here," Dandelion Salad Review "Finally, The

Truth About the Alamo," by Daniel N. White, Sept. 20, 2011.

—"An eye opening reappraisal of what really happened [at] the Alamo [and] Tucker's well researched account dramatically rewrites long-accepted history and shatters some of the most cherished and enduring myths of the 1836 battle," *Armchair General.*

—"Readers open to new interpretations . . . will find compelling arguments within its well-researched pages," *Dallas Morning Star.*

—"It is refreshing for historians to challenge the conventions of history," Army Magazine.

In reviewer Daniel N. White's words: "The elephant in Texas history's living room has always been . . . slavery," and Tucker has exposed this fact in full.

In his complimentary NEW YORK TIMES review (Nov. 10, 2016), Thomas E. Ricks praised PICKETT'S CHARGE: "Tucker, who has written many books of military history, makes the contrarian argument [but] the book is most interesting for the bright nuggets of information Tucker presents . . . a mosaic of thousands of pieces that, seen whole, amounts to a fascinating picture of what was probably the most important moment of the Civil War [with] new facts, different perspectives."

Indeed, most of all, Tucker's "New Look" books have provided a great many fresh insights about America's most defining and climactic turning moments of the nation's story. He has most often illuminated historical blind spots, while correcting "old school" narratives of America's most iconic moments. Even more, he has employed a host of new ways of presenting historical evidence to provide fresh interpretations and analysis of a groundbreaking nature.

Quite simply, decade after decade, Dr. Tucker has never written "your father's history" and never will. One professor emphasized Tucker's long-time role in shattering myths in multiple fields of history: "it is so good to know that we have academic warriors." The author's first-ever and award-winning biographies of men and women of all races and creeds have brilliantly illuminated the forgotten lives of underdogs, lost souls, rebels, outcasts, renegades, deserters, generals, Buffalo Soldiers, Tuskegee Airmen, pirates, misfits, nonconformists, and refugees, while going against the grain to reveal long-overlooked historical truths, forgotten narratives, and hidden history.

For example, Tucker has also presented an "unvarnished look" in his "ground-breaking new analysis at one of America's iconic battles" to completely overturn the long-entrenched traditional views, myths, and stereotypes, which have been falsely created. Consequently, EXODUS FROM THE ALAMO garnered "an exemplary series of reviews from objective publications and scholars" on both sides of the Atlantic.

In demystifying America's iconic turning point moments, Tucker's unique "New Look" perspectives of his books have allowed readers to rethink history and the overall human experience in an entirely new way. He has illuminated history in an entirely new light and from fresh perspectives to expose long-existing misconceptions and entrench myths.

The author's unique penchant for presenting unvarnished historical truths through an unfiltered lens has repeatedly overturned traditional history and generations of conventional thought, while revealing the truth about "taboo" perspectives long avoided by other historians. The author's groundbreaking books bring to life forgotten men and women long banished to history's most obscure margins, while bestowing credit and recognition where it is rightfully due.

AMERICA'S TOP ACADEMICS LAVISHLY PRAISE "NEW LOOK" BOOKS:

Tucker's PICKETT'S CHARGE has presented many fresh views and new perspectives to overturn generations of stale and obsolete Gettysburg history. This "magisterial" book about a turning point moment in American history during the most decisive battle of the Civil War has been highly-praised by America's top academics and leading Civil War and Gettysburg historians.

The *New York Times* review of PICKETT'S CHARGE praised the author's original and fresh approach:

—Tucker's "Pickett's Charge, A New Look at Gettysburg's Final Attack offers a vastly (and intriguingly) different spin on your average assessment of the presumed futility of the attack." *HistoryNet*.

—Historian Alan Axelrod, Ph.D.: "Phillip Thomas Tucker's magisterial Pickett's Charge: A New Look at Gettysburg's finally replaces 150-plus years of uninterrogated mythology with meticulously researched history to give us a new and long-overdue understanding."

—William C. Davis emphasized: "In his almost minute-by-minute account of the most famous infantry charge in history, Phillip Thomas Tucker provides a thoughtful and challenging new look at the great assault at Gettysburg, from planning to aftermath. Not afraid to lay blame where he thinks it belongs, Tucker is fresh and bold in his analysis and use of sources."

—Louis P. Masur, Distinguished Professor of American Studies and History, Rutgers University: "A thought-provoking and eye-opening study of this pivotal moment in American history."

—"the author does a workman-like job of revising many myths and misconceptions about the battle [and] takes issue with many of the long-held assumptions and analysis of the famous attack and seeks to revise many long-held misconceptions" Jerry D. Lenaburg, Graduate of the United States Naval Academy and Senior DoD Military Analyst, *New York Journal of Books.*

—"A popular historian deconstructs 'the greatest assault of the greatest battle of America's greatest war'," *Kirkus Reviews.*

—"No action in the Civil War is more iconic than the misnamed 'Pickett's Charge,' and yet few episodes of this most studied of wars is in need of more enlightened and enlightening reexamination [until] Phillip Thomas Tucker's magisterial Pickett's Charge," Alan Axelrod, Ph.D.

—"Pickett's Charge, A New Look at Gettysburg's Final Attack is a detailed analysis of one of the most iconic and defining moments in American history. This book presents a much-needed fresh look, including the unvarnished truths and ugly realities about the
unforgettable story," Press Release.

—"Tucker officers a fresh account of Gettysburg's final attack [and] reveals the tactical brilliance of a master plan that went awry. Drawing on ample primary sources . . . Pickett's Charge details the complexities and contradictions of one of the pivotal moments in our nation's defining contests." History Book Club and Military Book Club

—"Phillip Thomas Tucker's new book 'Pickett's Charge' . . . reveals the incredible Irish underpinnings of the day that changed America forever . . . Tucker sets out to quash two myths that have fueled Civil War debate for 150 years [and] The first of these is that Pickett's Charge was an ill-advised roll of the dice [and] The second myth is that Pickett's Charge, like the broader Confederate war effort, was Anglo-Saxon in its leadership and execution . . . Tucker introduces us to the Irish-born and the sons of the Irish-born" men of Pickett's Charge and "Tucker has restored a vital part of our history in America." *IrishCentral.*

DEATH AT THE LITTLE BIGHORN was still another History Book Club and Military Book Club selection like PICKETT's CHARGE and numerous other books by Dr. Tucker, including his recent ALEXANDER HAMILTON AND THE BATTLE OF YORKTOWN 1781 in 2022. These ground-breaking books have garnered praise for presenting a good many fresh perspectives and new views that have overturned the standard interpretations of generations of historians. In regard to Tucker's DEATH AT THE LITTLE BIGHORN:

—"Custer's last movements and decisions have been argued about since 1876, but, in my mind, no one has made a stronger case for what really happened [at the Little Bighorn] than Phillip Thomas Tucker," Robert Boze Bell, Executive Editor of *True West Magazine*, about Tucker's book.

—"Presents a fascinating, lively, and important reassessment of the famous Battle of the Little Bighorn . . . Where the 'Last Stand' happened and what it means will change dramatically for readers of this book." Clyde A. Milner, II, co-editor of *The Oxford History of the American West.*

—"Phillip Thomas Tucker [emphasized] that the true turning point of the battle came early with the charge at Medicine Tail Coulee Ford." *Wild West Magazine.*

ADDITIONAL ACCLAIM FROM LEADING EXPERTS:

Premier historian James M. McPherson, Ph.D., winner of the Pulitzer Prize and the George Henry Davis '86 Professor Emeritus of United States History at Princeton University, wrote how Tucker is "one of the most prolific Civil War historians" in America. Tucker's "PICKETT'S CHARGE" has continued his ground-breaking Gettysburg scholarship distinguished by new and original perspectives in groundbreaking words. The author's groundbreaking STORMING LITTLE ROUND TOP was described as "extremely well-researched and well-written," Choice.

Tucker's groundbreaking PICKETT'S and DEATH AT THE LITTLE BIGHORN (both History Book Club Selections) are "New Look" books that have presented a more inclusive approach, providing readers with a thorough and deep understanding of these pivotal moments in American history.

Talented historian Allen Carl Guelzo has also praised the author's books: "Phillip Thomas Tucker, who has written on topics as varied as the Alamo, the Revolutionary War, and African American soldiers [has produced a] narrative [that] is thickly sprinkled with commentary from diaries and letters."

In regard to Dr. Tucker's highly acclaimed BARKSDALE'S CHARGE at Gettysburg, Jerry D.

Morelock, Ph.D., emphasized how, "The author of the acclaimed Exodus from the Alamo does more 'myth busting' in this superbly argued book."

—Terrence Winchell, National Park Service Historian, emphasized how "Tucker has produced a wonderful addition to the library of the most discerning Gettysburg collector."

—Scholar Darryl E. Brock, Ph.D., also praised PICKETT'S CHARGE: "Presenting an exhilarating narrative based on rigorous re-interpretation of historical sources, scholars and lay readers alike soon recognize the Southern nation's high watermark as the second day at Gettysburg." In still another milestone study of a groundbreaking nature, Tucker's PICKETT'S CHARGE has continued his tradition of presenting "New Look" perspectives to correct stale Gettysburg historiography.

—Dr. Edward G. Longacre emphasized how "Burnside's Bridge highlights a significant but neglected aspect of Antietam [and] the author's scholarship is sound, his grasp of tactics sure, and his writing vivid, making Burnside's Bridge both a good read and good history."

—Likewise, the *Journal of Southern History* praised BURNSIDE'S BRIDGE: "Tucker offers a blow-by-blow account of the fight for the lower Antietam . . . Tucker deserves considerable praise for his efforts. Drawing upon a truly impressive range of primary and secondary sources, he has produced a thorough and highly readable narrative."

—William C. Davis, one of America's leading historians, wrote: "'The Thermopylae of the Civil War' . . . the single most remembered aspect of the fight, the contest for the bridge, has not until now been the subject of an in-depth book-length study. Phillip Thomas Tucker remedies this in *Burnside's Bridge* . . . In a work thoroughly researched and dramatically written, Tucker lays out the story" in dramatic fashion.

From BURNSIDE'S BRIDGE to PICKETT'S CHARGE that focused on the crucial eastern theater and to equally ground-breaking books about the western theater, Tucker has most often emphasized the most ignored and forgotten aspects of the Civil War. Tucker's books have illuminated the American experience to present multi-dimensional perspectives combined with groundbreaking narratives. Utilizing a rare ability to demythologize history regardless of the nation and century, Tucker has most often reinterpreted the outdated historical record and the most iconic moments of American history, while breathing new life into the outdated traditional narratives.

Dr. Tucker has long focused on exploring the most hidden history to expose misconceptions and correct the historical record long in need of fresh and new analysis for the 21st century. Tucker has presented the good, bad, and ugly of history by relying on primary documentation mined from little-known private and public collections, especially from Mexico, in his groundbreaking EXODUS FROM THE ALAMO. Tucker's EXODUS FROM THE ALAMO has also won widespread acclaim:
—"The research is hard to argue against [and] is pretty straight forward. Read all of it with an open mind before drawing your own conclusions. You just might surprise yourself." *Kepler's Military History.*
—"Exodus from the Alamo offers a fresh and fascinating look at [the Alamo and] Tucker's efforts to include all pertinent evidence, including that of previously

ignored Mexican sources, pays off in the form of a relevant and thoroughly researched book."
—"A necessary read for anyone interested in the Texas war of Independence." *Strategy Page.*
—"demonstrating a mastery and understanding" of the Alamo's mysteries. *Journal of America's Military Past.*
—"Dr. Tucker examines the real story behind the premier symbol of Texas . . . courageous as it is insightful, Exodus from the Alamo is a major contribution . . ." Antonio Zavaleta, Ph.D.
"I've just finished reading an extraordinary book, Exodus from the Alamo [from] reliable overlooked sources." *Present Progressive.*

Tucker has most often unearthed a good many long-overlooked aspects of ethnic and social history to significantly fill the wide cultural and social gaps in the narratives of America's story. Rewriting America's most iconic moments in great detail by relying on new sources of information, Dr. Tucker has brought vividly to life fascinating personalities in first-ever biographies about America's female Buffalo Soldier CATHY WILLIAMS (4 volumes); EMILY D. WEST; DAVID FAGEN (2 volumes); JOHN C. ROGINSON, FATHER OF THE TUSKEGEE AIRMEN; and four remarkable women of the HAITIAN REVOLUTIONARY WOMEN SERIES. Most important, all of these books have gained widespread praise.

—Professor Mario Marcel Salas, University of Texas, wrote: "Tucker knows how to mine the data for details lying well below the surface and use them to create an exhilarating narrative. This book demonstrates the power of analysis and the ability of the author to tell of the African American experience."

—Professor Tim Carmichael: "This engaging biography of John C. Robinson, the 'Brown Condor,' gives the aviation pioneer his historical due and . . . makes an important contribution to our knowledge."
— Edward G. Longacre, Ph.D.: "*Brothers in Liberty* recounts the long-neglected, historically and culturally important story of the free Blacks and mulattoes of Saint-Domingue (modern-day Haiti) in aid of American and French forces during the October 1779 battle of Savannah. The critical role played by the Chasseurs Volontaires in helping reverse the fortunes of the disastrous offensive against the British-held city has never been chronicled in such detail and with such deep feeling for the larger-than-military issues involved. Here is another characteristic effort by the Stephen King of American history."

Over a period of decades, Dr. Tucker has evolved into "the most innovative, hardest working, and diligently productive historian of his generation," in the words of one historian, for having authored more than 125 books of groundbreaking history. These books have brought many forgotten personalities vividly to life to illuminate the histories of many nations around the world by exploring remarkable lives.

Printed in Great Britain
by Amazon